The Initiate's Way

"All that proceeds from matter can beget only strife and all manner of conflicts between peoples as between individuals. The deeper one sinks into matter, the more the elements of division and opposition gain force and scope; and, contrariwise, the more one rises toward pure spirituality, the nearer one approaches that unity which can only be fully realized by consciousness of universal principles."

René Guénon
The Crisis of the Modern World

The author would like to offer special thanks to Christine Robins for her tireless efforts with proofreading and generally being an absolute star.

The Initiate's Way

by Jade Melany

© Jade Melany 2020

First Edition

All rights reserved. No part of this work may be reproduced, stored in a retrieval system, or transmitted in any form or by any means, electronic, mechanical, photocopying, recording or otherwise without the prior permission of the publisher.

Contents

Introduction by Richard Abbot	7
Esoteric vs Exoteric	9
Archetypes and Dreams	12
What do I mean by the term pathworking?	15
Fool: Awakening journey begins	20
Becoming the Magician or Magi	23
Magician	25
Awakening your Inner Goddess – High Priestess	34
Goddess of the Grove – Mother Goddess – High Queen	42
God of the Grove – Hidden god - High King	49
Shaman – Heirophant – Meeting your Inner teacher	55
The Lovers	65
Chariot of the Moon	75
Strength / Fortitude	87
Merlin The Hermit – Son of the Mother	93
The Wheel of Fortune and Fate	107
Justice – Change and transition phase	115
Drowned Man – Odin – Christed one	122
Death – Past Life Journey for Transformation	131

The Art of Temperance	138
Pan – Hermes – Devil	145
The Tower of Illusion comes crashing down	152
The Star Sothis	159
The Moon	164
Unconquered Sun	170
Judgement Call	177
The World (Change and transition phase)	186
How to read Tarot for yourself	192
Using Tarot cards to read for others	194
Major Arcana interpretations	196
Understanding the suits of the Minor Arcana	213
Minor Arcana/Pip Card Interpretations	218
Wands/clubs – spiritual influence	218
Suit of Swords/Spades – Thoughts	224
Suit Cups/Hearts – Emotions	233
Suit of Pentacles/Discs/Diamonds – Sensations	240
Understanding Court Cards	246
Index	259

Introduction
by Richard Abbot

It was some years into my professional Tarot reading career before I fully grasped the fact that Tarot cards exist as a bridge between worlds. This did not stop me reading the cards, as a divinatory exercise, either for myself or others, but this realisation did reorientate my approach and understanding of the cards and the process of reading them. Prior to this revelation I had used the cards to help clients navigate the events and situations of their life. The occultist William G Gray called these things 'Externalities', while my old occult teacher Arthur Norris called them 'Happenings in the Outer World'. Either way, these were the things that happened *to* people, outside of their being, and they often seemed all-consuming. Whether these things were school or family dramas, career anxieties, health problems, or social concerns they always seemed to take the client further and further away from themselves, and further and further off their path. I puzzled over this for a long time, and then the revelation struck me – Outer World (ordinary life) happenings were symptoms, not causes; they were symptoms of the state of our Inner World.

Gray termed these Inner World movements 'Internalities', saying '…Externalities exist only to arouse Internalities'. Put more simply, everything that happens outside of us can help us learn something about the inside of us. Gray continued, '…Internalities balanced against Externalities arouse Identification'. Again, more simply, when s*** happens in our life, so long as we are willing to work out its Inner World cause, then we may discover *who we are* and *what we are for. This is the Initiate's Way*.

When an individual (male, female, young or old) strikes out on their own – for example by leaving home, emigrating, starting their own business or leaving a tired relationship – they are acting in a Magician-like way. When a couple join together, sexually, emotionally, in mutual understanding, support and co-operation, they are acting in a Lovers-like way.

But these descriptions are much more than narrative associations. As far as I am concerned when such things happen in the Outer World it is because they have already 'occurred' in the Inner World.

Though this kind of thing happens to most people at some time in their lives, not everyone (indeed not hardly anyone!) will be conscious that *an Inner Shift always precedes an Outer Shift*, and that it is hardly ever the other way around. Who *is* aware of this fact? Initiates, that's who. People like you and me, freaks as far as most others are concerned, adventurers in Inner Space, on the quest to understand and ultimately master this Inner/Outer dynamic.

The Initiate's Way helps us greatly in this work, steadily drawing our attention toward the Inner World of meaning and causation, away from the Outer World of shadow-boxing and effects. For this contribution to a re-balanced perspective and a re-ordered world, they are priceless.

Esoteric vs Exoteric

A brief explanation for the terms "Esoteric" and "Exoteric" is presented here in order that the reader understand where I am is coming from in respect to this particular work. It is my view that a misreading of the word "Esoteric" has occurred when it is misunderstood as something hidden from all but a select few. Simply put anything that is "Esoteric" is that which comes from within, not from society, morals, politics, religion, or fashion. It is the thing that comes from the core of being within each individual. Whatever the mode of transmission it then appears in the physical world as expressions of art, literature, music, and poetry etc.

"Exoteric" is a general term relating to the experience of anything outside of oneself. I am suggesting here that religion itself is exoteric in the sense that there are sets of core fundamental beliefs attached to each religion whose source is outside one's self. Each individual, depending on their circumstances, life path, ancestry, and other life factors, may be drawn to, or repelled by one or more of the frameworks of exoteric belief systems.

> "Esoteric Art doesn't follow trends or movements in the arts. Chosen subject matter reflects the personality of the artist. The subject matter alters in the mind of the artist. It is influenced by memories, subconscious and conscious choosing. The artist is in a constant dialog with the subject matter and through this dialog it will evolve." – Tapani Moko (One of the Original founders of the Esoteric Order of Art movement)

The Esoteric Art movement or Order of Esoteric Art was initially founded by Tapani Moko and Marianne Kaunio in 2006, roughly around the same time as I began using the term Esoteric Art to describe the style of art I was painting. Their thesis succinctly described the process of creation that one goes through when creating esoteric art, and how the art arises from within the personality of the artist. The body of work I was engaged with at the time was entitled *Soulscapes*, so it was nice to discover others on the same page and that I had coincidentally used the term "Esoteric Art" around the same time that they founded their movement.

The Initiate's Way is a system of illumination, or pathworking using specific imagery during meditation or creative visualisation. There are twenty-two pathworkings which are based on the Major Arcana of the Tarot. The magickal images contained in this book emerged from my experience of the nature of Tarot and its function in everyday life, after using the pathworkings myself personally over a period of two years.

There are cyclical peaks and troughs over time in the pursuit of matters of an esoteric nature. Avoidance of this process is simply an opposing reaction towards our Western Culture and its generations, who are turning their attention increasingly towards technology and entertainment, rather than the natural process of getting to know themselves and exploring inner worlds. By using the pathworkings contained in this text the serious student will be able to break out of any patterns or limitations that may be holding them back by changing themselves from within.

What is it that truly makes us human, is it our gender, culture, beliefs? What makes us turn away from our inner world or core and concentrates all of our energy and attention into the external world or that which we see outside of ourselves? Somewhere along the way, our focus turned from within to living our lives in a purely exoteric manner and projecting an image of ourselves to others, rather than embracing the authentic or real personality that lies within each of us. One of the glaringly obvious things to come to light when I first set foot on my own journey, was the process of distinguishing between the inner and outer personality, and the part that belief plays in that process. Looking honestly at one's life and the surrounding influences, the happiness factors, and then analysing the true feelings about one's self and the relationship with the true self, or genuine authentic self. What are your true values? Can you even find them? Do they come from within or are they a replication of other people's ideas and opinions? These are some of the questions that inevitably surfaced for me at the beginning of the fool's journey. This quest was something that surfaced from deep within me at a particular crisis point in my life, and the experiences I had when working with the archetypes during pathworking, were priceless in terms of my own learning and self development.

At the simplest level, engaging with the Tarot imagery can facilitate self-healing and rid the mind of any toxic ideas or beliefs that may be holding back progression in life. It can help the practitioner to find meaning and purpose in life, while gaining control of the ship that sails through the murky waters of the mind, at the same time opening up to the endless possibilities of innate wisdom. If you are ready to begin finding out who you really are then, this book is for you.

Archetypes and Dreams

A word about Archetypes and awakenings is also necessary before any serious student of the Tarot sets out on their own journey of discovery. An "Archetype" in this work is an image associated with certain ideas, personalities, wisdom, mythical beings, gods/goddesses. It is a specific subject matter that has been represented in a symbol or in an image. In magical invocations and rituals if these energies are awakened then they become alive within the practitioner and this is what is meant by the term pathworking with the Tarot; to awaken within yourself these magical images and work with their wisdom and knowledge in the physical world.

The most important thing I would suggest you do before starting any work with the Archetypes is to get yourself a big hard-backed book of either lined or plain paper and keep it beside your bed, so that upon waking you can record any of your dreams and look back at them later for interpretation. We receive guidance that we need while we are in the dreamstate and once you start inner work you will find that you get intuitive dreams and bits of information, Spirit Guides also may introduce themselves to you first in the dreamstate. I personally don't think that the symbols that we receive in dreams have generic meanings, as we are all individuals, and a recurring symbol that one person dreams of could mean something totally different to another.

Start your own dream dictionary and take the time to meditate over the things that appear to you in your dreams and pretty soon you will start recognising patterns and know what to expect in the future.

"Tarot needs to come from within. Any Tarot I've worked on alone has always been meditated and drawn by me before I hand to artist! Stillness, listening, singing your way into the heart of things, watching the dreams, acting on them. I've done that all my life. But for most people, just plain noticing when this world and the other become apparent in the moments of insight: that's when you need to hold the stillness and not distract. Real art should make the hair on the back of your neck stand up with recognition. Imagination is a faculty of the soul, but it isn't the production of something imaginary, but a real window" – Caitlin Matthews

"Every image, however primitive it may be, leaves its mark. It evokes a memory, and only that which one has known or lived can be remembered. One puts into this image, "something" of oneself. The image no longer then represents this memory; it is the memory that is transplanted in the image."
– *The Temple in Man*, R.A. Schwaller De Lubicz

The Initiate's Way contains rites of passage in the journey of a spiritual seeker; internal pools or resources which you awaken within; experiences which can also open doors to other worlds, wisdom, knowledge that connects you with living archetypes and the lives and experiences of those who have travelled this spiritual journey before us. Like signposts or gateways, images can connect you with roads that you have yet to travel, and for the purpose of personal spiritual development, these are the foundations upon which you can build your new path.

Each image is one part in the whole process of the journey into enlightenment. By taking time to get to know each part of this journey intimately and experience it for yourself directly, you are taken out of the comfort zone of what you think you know, and you are awakened from within to a world of new experiences which then acts as a catalyst to bring change into your life. Pathworking with each archetype is not something that can be done quickly and requires time, effort and diligence on the part of the seeker and the act of meditating properly is a skill like any other which doesn't happen overnight, but with persistence and determination it is an invaluable tool that will yield phenomenal results if applied consistently and effectively.

I have called this body of work the *"Initiate's Way"* because the central core theme is based upon the idea of initiation through imagery and words, into the timeless wisdom and teachings in the Western Mystery Tradition. I cannot stress enough the need for rest, relaxation and learning to breathe properly to get the best out of this work. Learning to meditate is hard work and it is self directed.

You are literally training or sharpening your mind so that it will serve you as a functional tool for the rest of your life.

What do I mean by the term pathworking?

It is building up magical pictures in the imagination to introduce you to the archetypes and to experience the sensations that are invoked, guides you might meet, or visions that you may encounter. These are the main purpose of each of the pathworkings that I have written to accompany this series of images. Afterwards it is a good idea to record the different life experiences that you go through as you progress through the journey in much the same way as you would write a diary or journal about everyday life. Noting people that you meet in the real world, books you are led to, and oracles that you are drawn to, as these are all being brought into your sphere of existence by your inner working. Record these ideas, open yourself to receive more wisdom, and understanding, clarity and vision, so that your path in life may become clearly illuminated before you.

To get yourself into the frame of mind and state of relaxation which is required for you to begin this journey in earnest. I suggest you learn to breathe in and out to a steady count of four. Not as easy as it might sound, as your mind will wander as you inevitably start thinking about the events of the day or things that you think you need to do. Gently remind yourself, when your mind wanders, to focus on the simple task of breathing in and out to the count of four. If you are going to use this in a group setting, you can simply read aloud from the book, after talking the group into relaxation using this technique, with or without some gentle relaxation music playing in the background.

You might like to light a white candle in each of the four corners of the room to honour the directions and ask for your spirit guides, teachers and ancestors, and those who work with the light, to come in and assist you during your meditation. Frankincense essential oil in a burner or a few drops in bowl of steaming water will enhance the atmosphere. You can also adjust the lighting so it doesn't distract the eyes.

Opening before Meditation

"I call to the Guardians of the East, South, West and North to attend our (my) circle should it please them. I (we) am (are) here of my (our) own free will to work with Spirit in all of its forms, to honour the Goddess and God within and without. Spirit guides, ancestors elders, helpers, teachers, angels and those who work with the light please join me (us) in this evening (moment) so that I (we) can work together to strengthen the connection to the otherworld while we work in our Sacred Space.

Introductory Meditation

We are going to go within now and direct all of your energy and attention within your self. You are going to go deep inside yourself. Just listen to the sound of your breathing as you begin to count. I want you to push out your stomach as you breathe in and let it fall as you relax.

As you breathe in you count 1,2,3,4 and as you breathe out you also count 1,2,3,4. With every breath in you go deeper within your self and with every breath out you feel more and more relaxed. 1,2,3,4. Repeat this process for about a minute so as to give your body time to get accustomed to this breathing technique.

When you are breathing in a steady rhythm and you feel your body begin to relax, focus your energy and attention on the space just above the crown of your head.

Imagine that there is a bright white ball of radiating, swirling and pulsating light energy. Take as much time as you need to visualise this and when you can see it clearly or sense it, bring the white light down through the top of your head. See it clearly as it works its way down and begins to travel through your neck and along your spine. The light travels down your arms and reaches your fingertips. Visualise this white ball of energy clearing away any heaviness or tension in your neck and shoulders and sense the clear light as it moves through your back, cleansing you like an inner radiant shower.

Bring this ball of white light energy down through the base of your spine, spreading out into your hips and thighs, relaxing all the muscles and bones so that the legs feel like they are light as a feather. Imagine this ball of light coming down through your ankles and toes, softening all of the bones and releasing all the tension that they may have been carrying.

Once you reach the soles of your feet send the light energy down as far as you can until you connect with the core of mother earth. Then you are ready to begin.

See yourself standing high up on a hill with a cloudless blue sky above you and the heat of the midday sun blazing behind you. You feel alive, excited and free. There is a steep ravine behind you and you have a familiar at your feet waiting to tread this journey with you. As you stand up on this high place, take a moment to consider your journey so far. Where have you come from? Where do you want to go? In this moment you are free of all distractions and immersed totally in your spiritual body. Now a gentle breeze, like the breath of the earth, sends a shiver of excitement down your spine, and all of the tiny hairs on your body stand on end. Go now on your journey inward and when you are ready come back energised and ready to proceed.

Afterwards record any thoughts or sensations that came to you, any feelings that arose or any fleeting images you may have caught while you were in contemplation.

This is not a process that can be rushed and at best will take repeated attempts to gain a significant understanding of each archetype. If after doing this introductory meditation you would like to close your circle or sacred space until the next time you do inner work, you could say something like:

"I am grateful for all the wisdom and guidance received. In this space we connect with our hearts and even though the circle is open it is never broken."

Questions:

How does it make you feel to be standing at the outset of this journey? If there were any doubts or fears this is natural, spend a little time writing about your experience. If at any point you feel that this journey is not right for you at this time, wait until you feel that you are. When you are ready to proceed. Read on.

0 Fool

Fool:
Awakening journey begins

Images 1 to 10 in the cycle represent the first part of the spiritual journey which is much like that of the hero of the myths setting out on the mythical quest, except that you are going on a quest within to find something, and that something is YOU and your true nature. Each of these images have their own unique experiences and symbols. First you need to prepare the way for this experience and find out if you are truly ready to step on to your spiritual path.

This archetype is the seeker after experience, the innocence of youth, who, when they begin their journey into discovery, are consciously unaware that he/she carries within all of the answers to their own questions. Everything one wishes to know is already known if one would only look within. This archetype can be understood as an indicator that you are about to set off on an awakening journey seeking new experiences which are as yet unknown. The unknown is not to be feared, it simply means that you have no experience of it yet. Taking the plunge is a scary business to some, but rewarding once you are on the journey, learning, and seeking, bringing new experiences into your life. Imagine the cunning wild man/woman who converses with the birds and beasts, and is at home in the arms of nature or wandering aimlessly, seeking solitude away from the masses. Imagine someone living in the woods, and gathering what they need from the land around them, with a companion/familiar who would protect the wanderer wherever they would go.

The tendency to shallow breathe is often the first pattern which must be broken and reprogrammed to allow breathing from the abdomen. This achieves the desired result of a state of receptive and deep relaxation of body, so that you become accustomed to the necessary state of heightened awareness, and from there you can start your inward journey.

The fool has an expression of mischief on his face that is unmistakable. He is dressed in jester's garb, carrying a stick that has a 'wind bag' at the top of it. In his other hand he is gesturing as if to say, "are you ready to come with me on this journey?" There is innocence and mirth all rolled into one here and possibilities that have potential waiting to be released. As the seeker, do you have the courage to step out into the world and truly be who you were always meant to be? Are you ready to leap into the unknown?

The stance of the character is one of deliberately stepping out of the ordinary or mundane, becoming extraordinary to the point that one could imagine creating fire in their hands. Just like the flame of controlled passion of the artist, who ignites the spark of creativity bringing forth their manifestations into the physical world. The state of being associated with this archetype is one who is light on their feet, carrying no weight and treading lightly at the outset of a fantastic journey. The destination is as yet unknown but the foot had been firmly planted on the path waiting to jump.

Questions:

How does it make you feel knowing you are at the beginning of a great experience? Can you go with the flow and let things happen naturally? Where is your favourite place in nature? Can you visualise yourself there in your imagination as you sit in meditation? After the darkness of winter how does the stirrings of spring affect you?

Reflection:

Take all of the cards of the Major Arcana out of any Tarot deck that you work with and arrange them into three lines by laying them out on the table in front of you

1-7 on the top line, 8-14 underneath, and 15-21 underneath again. There is a story being told here, and if you look at them in this arrangement you will see three very different passages, through initiatory experiences on the journey towards enlightenment. Note anything that you become aware of in your meditation/dream diary and when you come back to look at this later you may be surprised at your intuitive reading of these images.

Becoming the Magician or Magi

This is the first step in the journey of getting to know who you really are and discovering your innate powers; your Will-power! You will need at least half an hour of undisturbed time to complete the pathworking, and make sure that you have your journal handy for recording your experiences afterwards. When you are ready get yourself comfortable and use the following to awaken within you your own personal power.

Close your eyes and begin to count your breathing. Remember to breathe in to the count of four and breathe out to the count of 4. Push out your abdomen as you breathe in. This may seem difficult at first but your body will remember that this is the correct way to breathe. When you breathe out, allow your abdomen to fall. Breathe in, 2 3 4 breathe out 2 3 4. Breathe in 2 3 4 and breathe out 2 3 4. Repeat this as long as is necessary so that you get the rhythm of the breathing and begin to relax.

Every time you breathe you feel more and more relaxed. I want you to begin your visualisation by creating a spinning ball of light just above the crown of your head. Imagine a light spinning and pulsating and growing from a tiny spark into a ball about the size of a watermelon. Spend a few moments imagining this ball of light until you can see it clearly in your mind.

When all of your energy and attention is focussed on this ball of light, begin to bring it down through the top of your head and to rest in your forehead for a moment.

You will feel any stress or anxiety dissolving as this ball of spinning light clears negativity and cleanses your thoughts, so enjoy this clarity of thought before moving on.

(Pause here)

Now bring the ball of spinning light down into your throat. Pause for a moment here and feel this clear light resolving any communication difficulties that you might have, allowing your confidence to grow and you will feel content that you can at any time, speak your truth.

(Pause here)

Enjoy this feeling of openness and comfort in the knowledge that you are ready to speak from within. Reflect briefly upon how you communicate with others. Are there times when you wish you could be more vocal about your true feelings and desires? Know that you can speak with confidence and be yourself.

Bring your attention back once more to the spinning ball of white light at your throat as it begins to move now down to your heart. As you become centred in your heart with this ball of energy connecting to the real you, the spinning ball of light begins to grow bigger and bigger until it envelopes your whole body.

A shaft of light emits from your heart down into the centre of the earth, connecting you with the core of our planet. You feel alive and radiant now within your power.

See yourself extending your arms outwards and projecting this energy, which is you, out through your hands, while feeling the light source streaming through you from above, and connecting you with the earth below. You are the creative spirit and this is your energy and willpower. You have energy in abundance. Allow it to flow freely and unrestricted. (Long pause here)"

When you are ready, come back to waking consciousness, feeling invigorated, alive, and centred within yourself. Write down any thoughts, feelings or intuitions received during your experience.

1 Magician

Magician

This magickal image shows the inner genius awakening and the will power focussed. Intent and desire are carrying this innermost energy of your individuality, from within to the external world. As you connect with your unique gifts and talents, whatever they might be, you can then go on to use this awakened force to do your Great Work. A clear inner voice is within reach, and if you listen very carefully, you can hear it speaking softly. It is a persistent voice within all the chaos of the chattering mind. After time spent in quiet contemplation it becomes louder and much easier to hear above the noise of the world.

During this part of the journey you will begin to understand that some of the things that you have believed or have been taught are at odds with what you innately feel inside, and that is perfectly normal. We often see portrayed in books and movies a wise owl companion that accompanies the magician: Harry Potter with Hedwig, Merlin and Archemides, and also certain goddesses such as Athena who are portrayed with owls beside them in their archetypical imagery. The Owl represents innate wisdom. If you think of your mind as a guide or inner teacher who travels with you into the shadowlands, with keen night vision and silent hunting prowess. It can assist you to unmask anyone around you that may be taking advantage or is attempting to deceive you. Mind chatter is usually the first obstacle that we need to overcome so that we can hear our innate wisdom.

The central figure of the magician is two forms at the same time. One in the background is standing with arms outstretched, wearing a blue robe. The second is standing with one hand reaching up to the sky, and the other directing the attention below.

The action being performed by the figure is that of bringing into balance and alignment the different parts of the self into one coherent whole, that will, once perfected, function as the driving force behind all of the creations that will manifest through the personality. The four symbols of the sword, cup, wand and disc are hovering within reach, and now you need to search deep within yourself, and discover these treasures for yourself, and learn to work with them. The magician is wearing an owl mask. The idea presented here is that by projecting masks that you create, it allows you as the magician to construct different personas. You will need these during the different life phases, so that you can play the game of life.

Think of this archetype as the entertainer whose light shines so brightly that those who watch are captivated in awe. A pure being that radiates from within; one who is in control of their own destiny and is the maker of their own fate. Unwilling to meekly accept what life has thrown at them, this archetype represents all of the pioneering spirits who see further than their own melodramas, and have the strength of conviction to create their own vision, and bring it to manifestation. The will to create is strong, and whatever those creations may be to others, they are the stuff of dreams, brought to life as the heart's voice begins to sing loudly for all to hear. This is the beginning and the end, the Alpha and the Omega, and a force that is cyclical in nature, driven by the imagination and willpower.

The cup, wand, sword and disc that appear on most magician Tarot cards somewhere represent the four suits within the Tarot deck, four elemental treasures, or four elements, and the four worlds from the Qabalah.

For this interpretation think of them as:

wands – spirit
swords – intellect
cups – emotions
discs – physical world

Also as elements symbolised in seasons of the year:

wands – spring
swords – summer
cups – autumn
discs – winter

Radiating your true self into the world and seeing things from a different perspective takes great courage and determination, so simply put, it is time for you to use your imagination and will power, to discover these worlds within, and integrate the experiences into your life. The way I did this personally was to work with one of the aces from the Tarot on my altar at the beginning of each season, to connect with the elemental energies.

> "The more en rapport the mind becomes with the inner spirit, the more perfect and symmetrical become these lines and the resultant forms" Adiramled *Divine Symbols*

A word on power is necessary here, for power alone corrupts, but power directed from the heart, and from a place of wisdom and knowing, creates stability, listens to reason, and considers all possible outcomes before action. Once the seeker finds out that they do not possess a soul, but that they are the soul, they realise the physical body has a limited amount of time on this earth, even though the soul of each of us is eternal.

The soul is the source of light for each individual, and if you turn the attention inward to experience this for yourself, your life will change dramatically. You have within you a radiating light, and as you change your perception to look through eyes newly awakened to the world, you can recognise the raw power that everyone holds within. The realisation that you are in charge of this power, allows you to create change. Sometimes lights will burn out unexpectedly, or electrical appliances go on the blink or develop strange technical faults, and generally there may be electrical disturbances until the newly awakened person begins to settle into this new awareness of personal power.

At this stage it is like looking into a magic mirror of one's own reflection, and in doing so, you can begin to discover the true nature within. Spirit reveals itself as an infinite entity, and you discover that you have choice in everything that you do. You have will and strength which allows you to develop the ability to open and close your consciousness, switching on and off the creative tap; once you have learned how to do it! Opening and closing of the mind, deciding what you allow or don't allow into your conscious awareness, you will begin to make decisions from a place of knowing.

Even though this may be a groundbreaking experience and realisation, you must remember that you are only at the beginning of the journey here. You take with you the experience of finding the light within, and over the course of the rest of the journey, you will kindle that flame to bring more and more of your true self into being. This is the fuel that keeps you going and the more you feed this part of yourself, the more you can turn inward in times of hardship and stress and lean upon this support that you have created for yourself.

This is the part of you that uses intense concentration and focus to carry through projects from inception to completion, like the saying, "Energy goes where attention flows." As you change your focus to tunnel vision, you are essentially blocking out unwanted distractions, until you have finished the task at hand. Once you have completed whatever it is that you have begun, you can then open back up to everything else. This stage of development is for you to learn to open and close your perception to the flow of information, incoming and outgoing, sending and receiving, being aware or choosing to restrict the flow of information that is allowed into your consciousness. You might be surprised just how much information filters into your subconscious without your knowledge of it!

Where does your imagination come from? How do you know when you are awake or asleep? When you dream is it to process the content that you experienced during the day or do you wake in order to explore the world around you, from within the creation of your dreams?

Become the magician and learn to create from a place that is your source of inspiration. This is a well which never runs dry, as it is inspiration that comes from within the Cauldron of your self. In recognising the four worlds in which we function as human beings, and aligning with them internally and externally, we can begin to progress on our fool's journey and take the tentative steps towards eternity.

Questions

Are you living your true destiny? Do you know what your life purpose is? Are the people who surround you the kind of people who support you in your decisions, or do you feel constrained by the opinions of others? Do you know yourself well enough to know where your strengths lie, and where you need to work on adjusting focus and clarity for the future? These are the things that you should meditate over.

Exercise

Whatever the season is now in which you have started your journey, select the Ace from a Tarot deck that represents that season. Place it in front of you and spend a little time looking at the imagery and think about how it relates to the element. Write your findings in your journal. This can be done at the beginning of each season until you feel like you have more of an understanding of each element.

Awakening your inner Goddess

As this is a night time meditation it may help to do this when it is dark, but if this is not possible, then block the light by putting something over your eyes. Total darkness is best for the desired effect. With or without gentle music.

It is a good idea to perform this pathworking at the time when the moon has just appeared in its crescent form, to fully appreciate the difference between the crescent and the full moon energies. The moon pathworking is very different to that of meeting the goddess/healer within.

Take a moment to bring your energy and attention within as it is time to go deep inside yourself. We begin by regulating your breathing and counting, and with each inhalation and exhalation you feel more relaxed. Breathe in to the count of four and then out to the count of four. Breathe in to the count of 4 then breathe out to the count of 4. Repeat this process until enough time has been given to get the mind into a peaceful serene state. Anywhere between 1 minute and 5 is good.

All around you is the dark blue of velvet midnight and you feel peaceful, calm and totally relaxed. Enjoy the stillness in this moment as you become accustomed to this twilight realm. Look above your head at the night sky. The deep midnight blue is pierced with tiny stars twinkling behind a misty haze. You concentrate and focus all of your thoughts on the sky and almost immediately the misty haze begins to clear.

A tiny sliver of a crescent shines down upon you and you smile inside at the horns of the moon revealed to you in this moment. You feel a gentle breeze and sense movement all around you but you can't tell where its coming from.

Taking your gaze away from the moon for a second you notice that the path underneath your feet is shining with a silvery luminescence. You feel the presence of another with you, though can't see her, but you feel her and you shiver with excitement. The path extends away from you and you can't see where it ends, but you feel compelled to follow it anyway. As if you are being guided by an unseen source. You begin to move. You are light on your feet as you travel along this sacred path.

You can hear the sound of running water and you notice that there are two streams either side of you, running parallel to the path. Keep walking and follow this path until you reach a waterfall. The two streams now both cascade over the edge of this moonlit waterfall, and as you look over the edge you see that they fall into a deep inviting pool a couple of metres below.

You hear a voice whisper to you that you have to trust your instincts and go down to this pool. How you get there is your choice, but know that however you make the leap, in a few moments you are going down to bathe in this sacred healing pool. So pause a few moments for the transition.

You feel the water against your skin. It is more wonderful than anything you have ever experienced before.

You feel cleansed, refreshed, and all of your cares, worries and concerns have gone. This is your sanctuary and you can visit as often as you like when you the need healing and peace of this moonlit pool. Allow memories to surface here, open yourself up to the whole of your consciousness and bathe in the stream of all that is you.

Take as much time as you need. When you are ready step out of the water. The air is just right. Not too warm and not too cold.

The gentle breeze against your skin makes you feel alive and you boldly walk back along the silvery path, taking with you all of your experiences. The presence of the horned moon guides you back along the path to where you began your journey underneath the night sky. Take a few deep breaths. Wiggle your toes. Stretch and open your eyes.

Write your experience into your journal and remember to leave it somewhere you can reach it in the morning upon waking, so that you can record any dreams that you remember. When recording dreams is is good practice to note the time of the lunar cycle, date and any significant symbols and recurring themes.

Awakening your Inner Goddess - High Priestess

The Divine Feminine Awakened, Source of inner wisdom

There is a bridge that you must cross at this point, in order to have access to the pool of wisdom that resides within, and for whatever reason, at some point in the past, there has been a disconnection from the divine feminine. At this particular point in the spiritual journey it is required that you make a giant leap across the abyss to reach the unconscious mind. So be prepared to look into this sacred mirror and accept all that is, with love and trust in your own intuition.

The experience here will bring you to new depths and higher dimensions, initiation into a different perspective and new way of seeing the world. Imagine looking out from behind the mirror with a view of everything without opinion, belief or influence of anything other than that higher part of consciousness that represents the truth in all things. The healer within steps forward and begins to direct life from a higher perspective and illuminates the darkness with each step outwards that she takes in to the world around her.

The Priestess of the Silver Star or High Priestess archetype, in terms of your journey into spiritual awakening, is the act of willingly retreating within to a place of healing and sanctuary. You must create this yourself, so that you can commune with your

2. *Inner goddess*

inner knowing and the ancestral pool of resources from which you originated.

The Gnostics call this archetype the goddess Sophia who is the embodiment of Wisdom. Your physical body is the temple through which you can receive the illumination of the Goddess and your vessel needs to be cared for with respect, dignity and love. It needs to be properly nourished on all planes of existence, physical, emotional, mental and spiritual. Listen again for that small but audible voice telling you what you ought to do, if only you would let it speak and be heard above the noise and chaos of daily life.

This is the realm of dreams, mystical states, otherworldly experiences and visions, and getting in touch with your intuition. In the stillness of silence turn the attention inwards and seek out that voice which speaks with inner knowing, and has waited a long time to be heard, acknowledged and awakened. As the inner goddess stirs from her long slumber, she brings with her an outpouring of innate wisdom. Here you are entering the realm of the female mysteries, and with that comes a deeper understanding of life and death cycles, and experiences in the physical world which are expressed as the triple goddess or the ancient image of the mother, maiden and crone. Wisdom, knowledge, and understanding are three very different things. Yes we can learn about subjects from a book of knowledge, but the book of life and its experiences are in a category all of their own. Sleep and dreams are a very important part of this journey and learning how to interpret the subconscious images and prophecies you receive, and distinguish between that which is the mundane and that which is pure knowing and intuition.

Knowledge can be transmitted through alternative means of communication other than verbal or written communication and this is what we are dealing with here. Take a Reiki attunement as an example of the transmission of non verbal consciousness from master to student. It is through the mode of non verbal communication we can awaken to ancestral consciousness and by tapping in to the shared pool of human experience, gain access to a succession of lives or a lineage of peoples who have walked this path before you and left behind a trail or a path for you to connect with. This image itself represents an initiation and an awakening and once you become aware of the reality of the inner world then you can begin to explore in more depth its shadowy realms, reaching different levels of understanding outside of that which you had previously known. (In my own case I had an awakening which was like a timebomb going off not long after a Reiki initiation with a lady, who coincidentally at the time was painting her own version of the three fates or the three faces of the goddess.)

The triple goddess Initiate's major life experiences, and as the 'mother' one of her initiations is associated with childbirth and the bringing forth new life into the world. But here we are presented with the face of the goddess as maiden which you can think of as connection with your virgin essence, or higher self, which once accessed is the vehicle through which the wisdom of the High Priestess flows. The third aspect of the goddess as the crone we will discuss later, as it is she who goes by many names and stands as guardian at the opposite end of the cycle. She draws everything to a close at the end of one journey and highlights the crossroads for the next stage.

The 'silver star' is Isis personified in her role as mother, wife and sister and in some traditions she is the star of Venus shining radiant beauty out into the world from within an awakened individual. One who has had a brief glimpse through the veil and has come back with a deeper understanding of life, death and the journey.

When you have reached this stage in your spiritual journey, you can begin to think of your soul as being self created from the heart, and that a spiritual journey into a deeper, and more meaningful existence can only begin with the recognition of and connection with your inner goddess.

Latent psychic abilities awakening are likely to occur at this stage and they may start to manifest in the form of prophetic dreams or waking moments where you just "know" what is going to happen next. The wilful exploration of other realms of existence other than the physical such as shamanic journeying, vision questing, deep meditation and pathworking to name but a few, are likely to be a consideration of the practitioner at this time. She is the archetypal image of the healers, empaths and clairvoyants of whom are in tune with subtle realms and this is the beginning of walking a path of balance guided from within.

The emphasis here is the need to create a quiet, healing, and sacred space that you can retreat to. If you don't have a place like this in your home then you must create one, or find a suitable place outside in nature where you can go to recharge and rest. Is there a place you like to visit in nature that makes you feel better?

Do you like to hear the sound of running water to relax or do your prefer to hear the breeze as it rustles through the leaves? Pick somewhere that feels sacred to you. Wherever it is that you feel most relaxed, safe and secure, make an oath to yourself that you will spend a little time there regularly in quiet reflection, whenever you can, as it will aid you in dealing with life's stress and strain. Peace comes from within and more often than not, you will be running around after others in times when you should be taking some reflective time out, perhaps to avoid dealing with the emotions and turmoil that you have within.

In the long run all the hurt and pain that you try to hide from others by burying it inside yourself, and also trying to hide from yourself by burying it even deeper, will surface and manifest eventually. So its better to deal with it head on in the safe space of a healing sanctuary that you have created, rather than the aftermath of an exploded can of worms. Anytime you need to, return to your healing sanctuary and visit this space where you can look deep into this pool of innate wisdom. The High Priestess holds the keys to a secret doctrine that can only be experienced and explored within you. Some representations of this image, like Juno, or Sophia are the personification of divine wisdom, or the female heirophants of the mysteries. Part of her essence is veiled and is such because we must learn to traverse the abyss in order to reach her.

Questions

Are you in touch with your intuition? Do you "know" instinctively what to do when something isn't right? Can you feel with senses other than those used in the physical world? Can you access your inner wisdom, to help you through difficult phases in life? Is your sanctuary prepared so that you can retreat within in times of need?

Connecting with the Goddess of the Grove

Take in a nice deep breath and while doing this push out your abdomen and close your eyes. Let out the breath slowly and the abdomen will fall naturally with the breath, begin your fourfold breathing using this same technique of pushing out your stomach when you breathe in and letting it fall when you breathe out. Breathe in to the count of four and on the out-breath of four your body remembers that it is time to relax.

Breathe in 2,3,4 and breathe out 2,3,4. Repeat this for at least a minute so that the body has time to fall into the natural rhythm of the breathing. Bring all of your energy and attention deep inside yourself. You are going within now to connect with the very essence of everything that makes you human, and with every breath you feel more and more relaxed. Upon every breath you go deeper and deeper into your self, and any noises or distractions around you fade away into the background as you become connected within yourself. I want you to send all of your energy and attention down, this time right through the soles of your feet.

Connecting with the Goddess of the Grove

You are reaching for an energy that you can sense deep within the core of the earth, so keep pushing down until your awareness moves through the ground underneath your feet. Your awareness travels down so far that you feel as if you have reached the very centre of the planet earth, and you feel safe here in a shell, protected by the earth mother.

This is the seed of you planted deep in the darkness from which you will grow. You feel a strong presence growing with you here inside this tiny shell, and at the same time you are aware of the earth and all of its living inhabitants; Trees, animals, flowers, birds, bees, and insects. You are a spark of life germinating in this tiny seed from the same source as every other living being and mother earth is giving you all you need for your journey.

Feel yourself growing roots out of this tiny seed and you begin to grow shoots like a tiny sapling seeking light in this dark nourishing environment. Feel the tendrils of your roots extending out into the soil and growing stronger by the second. You feel alive, literally bursting with energy in abundance. You hear the noise of raindrops tapping on the surface of the ground way above you and know that you have to strive upwards now towards this moisture. Use all of your strength and yearn for the surface of the earth once again.

You reach the surface and break through the soil just in time to catch a glorious rain shower to nourish your thirst. You draw the water in through every pore until the rain ceases and the wind blows around you, whispering through the leaves of grass in your shared space in this meadow. Golden rays of sunlight pour out from behind the break in the clouds and you bask in the glory of living. Time is endless here and your journey has just begun, so little by little you begin to grow alongside the creatures, flora and fauna in this blissful paradise and you feel your connection to the earth strengthening day by day. Spend as much time as you need here before you begin your journey back to everyday waking.

Bring back with you all of your experiences and make a note of anything significant that you felt during your experience.

Goddess of the Grove - Mother Goddess - High Queen

Goddess of the Grove

This radiant figure of the Goddess of the Grove looks very much like one of the antique rounded sculptures of Venus, and she is one of the Guardians found in myth as the figure of Demeter. This goddess is the embodiment of the Great Mother who nurtures you during your time on this planet and every time you visit nature you can connect with her and recall that as creatures we are indivisible from nature. When born on to this planet you share your existence with the flora and fauna and humans have connection with everything on the planet and in their lives. Your life, certainly the spiritual experience, is dictated by that cycle of life energy that comes from the sun. You can journey alongside the path of the sun, as it strengthens and wanes during the seasons. When the planet comes back to life and re-awakens in the springtime, you too awaken from a long period of darkness and introspection and at the other end of the cycle a part of you retreats peacefully back within, to its slumber during the winter months.

This archetype is the Mother Goddess who rules in her own world and represents that part of you that is connected with every other living entity on this planet. She is "Love" in all of its forms and abundance, and she guards the mysteries and rites of passage that come with child bearing and child rearing. She becomes the

3. *Goddess of the Grove*

embodiment of the personality in full bloom unswayed by external influences, one who is centred within their own self-awareness.

The Goddess is humanity in the bigger picture. Your connection with the Mother Goddess puts you in touch with the compassion and kindness within yourself, and illuminates the sense of union with your fellow travellers. She promotes understanding and integrity, and how to be without judgement, as after all we are in this world together, and a world without compassion and the sharing of love leaves no room for growth or maturity.

> "She is the empowered heart, at one with herself, independent, creative, loving, stable, abundant, nurturing herself and others." Chesca Potter *Greenwood Tarot*

The Mother Goddess guards the entrance point into greater mysteries, in the sense that through her you can birth yourself into a greater understanding of the divine feminine, especially once you have symbolically or ritually gone through the chamber of her to bring to life your "Soul". There has been a deliberate repression of the female aspect of deity for centuries and in today's society God subsequently became associated with a masculine force. Here we are presented with the full bodied and shapely goddess Venus, whose image was fashioned into figurines, and carved into stones in aeons past. She was carried by pregnant mothers to ensure their unborn children a safe passage in to the world, or kept in the home so that the goddess would bless the household. She is just as important as her counterpart and should be honoured within and without.

Numerologically 3 is indivisible by anything but 1, and 3, so if you look at this archetype as a culmination of three different individualities represented by 1,1,1 or as three different parts synthesized into one. When studying the idea of the trinity we can begin to scratch the surface of just how important this image and number have been, especially in terms of cults and religious movement over the centuries. The rise and demise of Mother Goddess cults and the use of the Triskelion in religious and spiritual symbolism.

In R.J. Stewart's work on the Merlin tradition, he writes about the three-in-one having female and male archetypes, that represent stages or transitions in the spiritual journey. If you take this archetype as being the first of three feminine aspects of being, you can recognise the archetypal mother, maiden and crone, having their balance or polarization in the male figures of the child God, the King and the Mad Seer. Somewhere along the line this triplicity seems to have been confused permanently into the God, The Father and the Son, but it seems there is a healthy resurgence and re-awakening of the goddess traditions in spiritual groups and gatherings. Consider the relationship between mother and child in spiritual and religious iconography, and take some time to explore the ancient Myths.

What about the archetypical Mad Seer and the Old Hag/Crone? These are initiations into different stages of progression or growth in the the life cycle of humans, and to understand this process fully is to consider what each stage represents, and imbibe the lessons that come with it.

Exercise

From the 22 Major Arcana, which archetype do you feel you might resonate with the most in terms of where you are currently in your own spiritual development cycle? Lay all of the Major Arcana out before you and pick one in particular that you feel most drawn to? Write your initial thoughts or feelings evoked when looking at the image. You can come back to this when you have learned more about each of the images and see what your initial thoughts and feelings were, in comparison to what you learn on your journey.

I painted the *Goddess of the Grove* after participating in the pathworking presented here. When I went down into the earth to connect with the Mother Goddess I saw this image, poised at the entrance to the cave of the mysteries. In my own meditations and studies I had found a place within that I could retreat to and she was guarding this sanctuary grove. A direct connection with the earth mother and the life force that flows through us all. Retreat into caves as a place of worship predates the creation of buildings and sanctuaries and, I believe, connects us to an older stream of spirituality that was natural to our ancestors.

Around the time of painting the *Goddess of the Grove* I remember dreaming about a cave that had various sacred ritual objects scattered on the floor from all eras in history. I remember feeling the presence of the Goddess as something unmistakeably magical and timeless.

The cave that the goddess of the grove is guarding contains an underground stream, or the source of spiritual traditions that lie just underneath the surface of perception. They are there if you know where to look and if you are not afraid to seek for the light in the darkness.

Regeneration and rebirth through the goddess come only when the seeker has no fear of the unknown, or of embracing the dark because nothing can grow from the light alone. Follow your own roots down deep and connect with the mother of us all. Take time to get to know her and listen to breath of the Earth as she nurtures us while we grow in the school that is life on this planet.

Questions:

How does it make you feel when you think about your relationship with your own mother? Do these feelings and thoughts have a positive or negative influence on the way you live your life? Were you nurtured or neglected as a child and what, if anything, would you change if you could? How do you feel when you are out in the wilds in the natural world? Spend a little time journalling about these questions and seek out some places in nature that are sacred to you. Listen in the spaces between the moments, what can you hear?

God of the Grove:
Hidden God; High King

Make sure that you will not be disturbed for at least half an hour and make yourself comfortable before you begin.

Breathe in to the count of four and breathe out to the count of four. Remember that when you are breathing in you push out your stomach and and let it fall when you are breathing out. Breathe in 2,3,4 and breathe out 2,3,4. Breathe in 2,3,4 and breathe out 2,3,4. When you breathe out you begin to feel more and more relaxed. Breathe in 2,3,4 and breathe out 2,3,4. Bring all of your energy any attention into yourself. Your body is comfortable and keep your focus on your breathing.

I want you to imagine that you are standing in front of a big window. There is light streaming through the window and you turn to warm your back with this radiant sunlight. You feel an intense rush and surge of energy coming towards you through the glass. It burns with an intensity of which is generated in an open fire.

Feel that fiery source as it enters through the crown of your head, radiating down the back of your neck and pulsating down your spine. The heat travels through every cell of your body as the fire moves down your back and spreads out through your shoulders, down your arms and to the ends of your fingers. Feel the fire as it moves through your lower back, and your hips, travelling through your legs and coming out of your toes.

The heat feels good, almost therapeutic and as you walk away from the window that is still radiating that heat, you bask in this inner fire. I want you to take a good look around you now until you find a door.

What does your door look like?

Remember all the details of the door. What is it made of? Is there a handle? Your body still feels as if you are on fire as you walk up to the door. I want you to visualise yourself knocking on that door. After a moment you hear a loud click and the door swings open wide. Through the gap you see a brightness that hurts your eyes momentarily. You feel the presence of a god, hidden to you before this moment. From within the sun he speaks to you as you walk through the door and out into the bright sunlight. Here is his living presence embodied in the spirit of nature. Pause here.

Your spiritual body has been cleansed and purified with a Spiritual fire. Burning away any negativity or self doubts, clearing the way for your growth. I want you to walk out into the open landscape now, and as you do fine droplets of rain begin to fall upon you, and a gust of wind blows through you which you inhale deeply. The radiating heat within you begins to subside as the droplets of rain cool your temperature. You feel alive and refreshed by the rain and the wind that blows around you clearing away any dust and debris from your purification.

Take a few moments to ground and centre after your experience. Write down your experience in your journal.

4. God of the Grove

God of the Grove - Hidden god - High King

Here we meet the Green Man who is the face or emblem of the spirit of nature. Of all the images that we have looked at so far this figure grounds you into the element of Earth. Awakening this archetype is to make a connection with the hidden god who is the counterpart or partner to the goddess. Where she is open and receptive he is active and energetic. You must seek the middle ground between these two archetypes to achieve the desired balance between domesticity, work, play and rest in your life.

The image projects a strong dominant personalty and is a personification of those who are brave, fair and vigilant in their work lives, warm and sensuous in their home lives and who lead an equally balanced life between work and their domestic environment. He is an image of active cultivation of leadership qualities of those who are determined to succeed. He is representative of building a secure future and considering everything that comes with the act of living in the modern world such as working for the money you need to thrive, and paying attention to administration, finance, business and ultimately power in its most raw sense.

At the bottom of the image there is an equal armed red cross whose ends taper into the *fleur de lys*, and it is the focal point where all the different energies and colours are being drawn towards it and being whirled about by it, much like the action of the fylfot cross (sun wheel) of the Tibetans. The four points of the equal armed cross on its own is a worthy subject for meditation, to understand its deeper significance and the power of the glyph, its origins and its use in magic.

Astrologically the God of the Grove is associated with Aries and the great awakening in springtime as the sun gains strength after its slumber through the cold dark of winter. Think about the cyclical process that you share with the Earth during your spiritual journey. During the pathworking you can undergo the wilful process of refining your personality, as a metaphysical burning away and purification by fire of those things that no longer serve you. If you can transmute negative personality traits, what you are left with afterwards, is a clear channel through which you can direct and focus your power.

Numerologically you could consider this stage in the spiritual journey in two ways. 4 is divisible by 1 so you can look at this as a human being having a fourfold nature, in other words divided into emotional, spiritual, physical and mental parts. Each is a separate entity in its own right and when reconciled, make up the whole that is the human being. The symbol of a cross within a circle suggests these divisions and acknowledgement and understanding of these parts, and the whole that they make up, is an important part of the process of discovering our gifts and talents. Numerologically as 2 + 2 which is the High Priestess archetype to the power of 2, then this stage in the journey allows you to create a solid platform upon which to rest your wisdom, knowledge and understanding and grow your true nature into being in the physical world and into manifestation. A cleansing or purification of the personality is required to remove any toxicity, clearing out of habits and negativity that can cause blockages.

Finally exploring the archetype numerologically as the numbers 1 and 3 could be viewed as the creation of an opposing nature, or viewpoint. The belief in one Godhead birthing an intolerance towards the Gods and Goddesses of the many which we so often see in religions of the 'one' god.

This archetype also suggests a figurehead that is perhaps idealistic rather than realistic. So taking into consideration the previous three archetypes and their significance at this stage in the spiritual journey there is a coming together, a recognition of the fourfold nature of the human personality and the integration of these allowing you to function as a singular whole, rather than from one of the previous four archetypes.

The square or cube is also associated with this image, as is everything that has a solid form, including the physical world, objects, people, animals, vegetation, and life lived out on the Earth plane. I would also put time in here and everything that happens in the mundane world, as well as a recognition of cyclical time as the beginning of an important stage in the process of self-awareness.

The inner transformation at this point in the journey is metaphorically linked to the sun gaining strength after the spring equinox, little by little the sun gets warmer leading up to the burning heat of late summer. Inner strength is discovered, revived and gradually the self becomes more assertive, not aggressive, but more surefooted. Knowing where to go, who you are and projecting your inner power into projects and your work and creating success in the physical world.

It is about manifesting a life that is true to one's inner being and burning away all the negativity, self doubts or limiting beliefs that may hold you back and prevent you from having total faith in your abilities.

Learning how to wield one's power and be assertive, shouldering great responsibilities, as would a benevolent ruler such as the mythical King Arthur, archetypical supreme ruler, being King within one's own world and ruling one's self well.

Questions:

Do you lead in your own life or are you happy to follow others? How do you feel about authority figures and the relationship that you have with your own father? Do you have the courage and inner convictions to live your life as you choose and still be able to fulfil your familial responsibilities and duties?

Shaman – Heirophant – Meeting your Inner teacher

Once again I want you to focus your energy and attention within your self. I want you to go deep inside yourself. All the distractions around you fade away into the background as you begin your breathing. Breathe in to the count of 4 and breathe out to the count of four. Remember to push your stomach out as you breathe in and let it fall as you breathe out. Breathe in 2,3,4 breathe out 2,3,4 and continue this until the mind chatter has subsided.

Now I want you to imagine that you are walking through an old oak woodland. The scent of moist damp earth fills your senses as you walk through these beautiful old trees. The breeze whispers through the branches as you walk along the path through the dense forest.

You hear birds singing and what sounds like a voice in the distance calling your name. The ground is hard underneath your feet and the air is warm despite the breeze. You can hear the sound of cows braying from a field somewhere behind you. Ahead of you there is an opening in the trees and you feel a pang of excitement because you have never seen this part of the woods before. As you stand in the gap of the trees looking through a shaded tunnel of leaves, you can see a clearing beyond.

Make your way towards the clearing.

As you walk through the tunnel into this space you notice that all sounds seems to vanish and an unearthly silence closes in on you.

You are surrounded by circle of majestic tall grey stones. You walk into the middle of the stones and stop for a second to take in the deep blue of the cloudless sky above your head. This looks like the perfect place and as you reach the centre of the circle you see that there is a seat roughly hewn from a large block of stone and you sit down in it. You feel so calm and peaceful and serene in this place. Immerse yourself in the air, feel the warmth of the sun and the feeling of the grass underneath your feet.

The heat of the sun makes your body feel as if it is floating and sinking at the same time. Every single cell begins to release any stress and anxiety that it was carrying, it just dissolves with the sunshine against your skin. Call now to your wise inner guide and tell them that you are ready for them to come and speak to you. Take some time in this moment to listen to their guidance before returning to waking consciousness.

5. Shaman – Heirophant

Shaman – Heirophant – Meeting your Inner teacher

This magical image emerged as a wise inner teacher, an archetype of a priest/shaman or wise old man. It is at this stage in your spiritual journey you must call to your inner teacher to step forward and guide, to act as interpreter to the endless source of ancestral wisdom that lies within you. You are the product of the generations that have gone before and all of their wisdom runs through your veins.

What we are dealing with here is the birth, or re-birth, of wisdom consciousness that you have somehow been disconnected from. After your pathworking and meeting with the inner teacher, you should learn to focus and listen to the guidance and instructions that you receive. Journalling the thoughts and ideas that come to you. As you learn to trust the intuition and have the faculty of knowing it is a reliable source of guidance. You can now stop looking outside for answers and realise that you have all of the answers within.

The significance of the character represented here will differ with each Tarot artist based on their inner beliefs and culture. The title Heirophant in some decks could suggest a connection to Christianity or Catholicism but this archetype suggests a different stream of tradition. It is entirely focussed on the emergence of wisdom from within the student rather than the seeking of an external teacher, and highlighting the importance of lessons that you can learn from nature as your teacher.

The astrological connection is with the sign of taurus, or the element of fixed earth. Think about the period in history when agriculture came into being, and the hunter gatherers who worked with the land. Peoples who were down to earth, connected with nature, living in harmony with the planet and innately understanding seasons and cycles that we have as a culture become increasingly disconnected from in the advent of technology. It represents a very different culture from that which we find ourselves in now.

If you look upon this Archetype as a part of yourself, that requires regular attention and treat it as you would any other human relationship. You can develop a conversation of sorts which will allow you to make decisions based solely on your innate wisdom. By visiting ancient sacred sites and places of worship associated with these times, there is much power, wisdom and knowledge in the land residing with its guardian spirits.

Perhaps you may find yourself developing an interest in herb lore and preparations of potions and remedies, or beginning to research your own roots and traditions within your family. There is a great emphasis here on the need to spend much more time aligning with the natural world, and spend some time listening to the wisdom of all of the great philosophers and sages who have walked the earth before you. Is there a particular subject that interests you, but you haven't had the time to explore? Are you drawn to a particular speaker or author?

The Heirophant/Shaman is the archetypical wise old sage who has travelled extensively and sought the external as well as the internal mysteries, presented here as an inner teacher. The keys that can be found on lots of traditional images for the Heirophant suggest the ability to open a gate. The gate that is the doorway into your own personal paradise. Institutions of learning are commonly found to be a consideration in life when this card appears in a reading, or that there may be a need for some spiritual guidance in one form or another. You could go so far as to say that that communion with this Archetype offers the key to understanding faith.

> This card signifies the initiate or master of the mystery of life and according to the Pythagoreans, the spiritual physician. Manly Palmer Hall. *Secret teachings of all ages*

The previous image of the *God of the Grove* was very much focussed upon the solar aspect of God-Consciousness, whereas this image is more aligned with the lunar cycles, agriculture, and the passage of the seasons, farming, animal husbandry, the land, ley energies, and the laying of foundations or building of a belief system. One which is truly connected with Mother Earth and that plays a part in building bridges or relationships between opposing forces. Words, poetry, ritual, ancestral heritage, and initiation rites are all key phrases associated with this stage in the spiritual journey.

> The word Druid comes, according to one etymology, from the roots 'Dru' – an oak – and 'id' – to know or be wise. And so a Druid is an 'oak sage' – a 'forest sage' – someone for whom the forest is their church.
>
> Philip Carr-Gomm. *Pagan Christian Planet Earth*

Thinking of this archetype as representing the teacher, the system and the way, then the baby image on the back of my previous deck, the *Soulscapes Tarot*, is very significant, as it magically gave 'birth' to that particular set of images. At the time of creating that deck, the back image represented a newly awakened part of consciousness, one that I was beginning to form a relationship with at that time. I was accessing inner wisdom and inspiration.

During the process of birthing that inner guide, I was researching and reading a lot about the Merlin of Britain. The Shaman Heirophant in this set of magical images was the last to emerge, and he acts as an overseer, and has been my constant companion throughout the rest of the uncharted waters of the journey of teaching the Initiate's Way to others. You hold in your hands now the keys to unlock your inner nature from its cage or prison. Mythologically speaking you release your Merlin from his enclosure!

> The original institution of British Christianity was the Celtic Church... its saints... were heirs to the Druidic tradition... they rejected the formalism of established [Roman] religion and returned to the source of the religious spirit in the wild places of the countryside, for several centuries Christians and pagans lived side by side.
>
> John Michell, 2008, pp.12. *New Light on the Ancient Mystery of Glastonbury*

On a deeper level still, there is a lineage or tradition being suggested here which definitely originates in the British Isles. It was almost extinguished, apart from the oral traditions, some of which still thrive today, despite the repeated attempts at extinction by those who wanted it to disappear.

We can easily make connections between this image of the Shaman/Heirophant to that of the mythical Taliesin "Master of the Mysteries", as an extremely ancient old man. For a more indepth study of this, I refer you to "The Third aspect of the Three Faces of Merlin (youth, maturity, old age" in R.J.Stewart, *Merlin Prophecies*. The idea is that this archetype becoming the figurehead of a tradition, or the father figure of a branch of knowledge that lives on through the folk traditions and customs, associated with guardianship of the land and nature. Taliesin the Bard was also known as the sacred Ox and the beginnings of the Celtic Church, which in parts is indivisible from Druidism. So again this image portrays a lineage of spirituality that is rooted in British Culture. In its evolution it may have gone on to birth Christianity and other ancestral spiritual pathways. The idea of the Celtic Underworld, Heaven, The Isle of the Apples, and the Pagan Summerlands, all have characters who journey through the shadows in their quest bring forth "inspiration". At the end of their quest, their journeying has been for the sake of enlightenment and not for material gains. It is too deep to go into in detail in this present book, but perhaps the history of conversion of the "unclean" Pagans to Christianity may not necessarily be the whole truth.

In the Rider Waite/Pamela Coleman Smith version of this image, there are two figures kneeling in apparent servitude in front of an elevated figure, or one who has been 'enlightened', and perceived to be upon a pedestal as one who "knows" and has experienced and gained control over the known and unknown universe, within and without.

In summary this archetype relates to the path of an individual who is answering to a higher calling, and is no stranger to the pursuit of knowledge, as they have chosen their path already and are strong in their beliefs. Organised religion may be the path for some and solitary seeking for another. Whichever path is chosen will be the right one for the individual concerned and those who would seek to give guidance to others, should be prepared to be open to different ways of thinking and learning and know that their way may not be for everyone!

Questions

Is there a particular spiritual tradition that you feel instinctively drawn to? Do you feel more comfortable taking part in groups or alone when it comes to religious or spiritual matters? What is your family or ancestral religion or spirituality and are you actively engaged in it?

> The historical character (of Merlin) – Merlin's Madness after the battle of Arderydd fled to the woods and lived as the Wild Man in the Forest. Historical accounts of Merlin tell us that after his sojourn in the woods he went into a monastery and was converted to Christianity. This image could psychologically represent a breakdown of sorts like "the Merlin in his wild feral state", representing the drop outs who refused to follow the Roman system, the survivalists keeping the flame alive. The wild men who live in the woods. The wild man and the wild woman living in the woods representing the horrid past, or the alternative to Roman Christianity. Son of the Devil and Servant of God according to Geoffrey of Monmouth. Half Pagan half Christian. Who was he working for really? Perpetuating the undercurrent of Druidry and Pagansim, threads which is why it was never completely stamped out. (Ragnarok/Armageddon) Dark ages when the laws of Rome collapsed, time of enlightenment or shadow. The bright light being the European Paganism of the Norse Vikings. The Shadow upon Roman Christianity and Roman Law. Merlins influence shows the power of one human individual and what they can Achieve.

Britain's other name is "Merlin's Enclosure". Mythically encountering Vivienne and being trapped in an invisible prison, a system or a process, or a methodology that is unknown to others, other than the Adepts or the Initiates within the system.

It is an invisible college to the rest of us. The invisible prison is Druidry, or Druidism, the Old Faith which continues to this very day in secret. They did not vanish they just went underground. The flame of Druidism has never died out. Knowledge is absolute power. Retention of Knowledge is vital. – Thomas Sheridan, "The Velocity of Now" (Youtube June 10, 2015)

I wrote the following poem concerning the Merlin mysteries during my first visit to Northern France, during which I had spent a large part of summer 2011 in meditation in the old oak forest near my parents home,

Wild man of the Woods
I seek the wild man of the woods, wise man of the mound
I seek the wisdom of the serpent buried under the ground
My heart lies in Avalon and in days that are LONG GONE
Whispers in ancient dreams and Wisdom in two streams,
The Red and the Green
The Earth's blood I hear
Humanity has fallen into war on consciousness,
Wicked men who seek to keep us in
The dungeon of the unknown
From which there is no return

Answers and guidance I seek
Lead me to where I can see
The door with the hidden key
That bars the way for those who lie
Their true nature withers and dies
Archetype of all that's Wise
I do not fear the Serpent
or the fire within its eyes
An alchemical messenger brought me
To the hidden observer
Through the mirror, the looking glass
That goes on forever
    Standing on the shoulders of giants
In the land of the ancients
The forest speaks in tones and hues of evergreen
The noise radiates from without and within

A pulse, a frequency
A realm in its own right
Opens up before me as I seek in the Twilight
A path stretches out
Following a silver thread
Soft gentle Moonlight
The quicksilver and the lead
The cauldron of the self
Ready to rebirth the phoenix, the lion and the eagle
    and ride high upon their Magick

21st August 2011

The Lovers*

After finding your centre grounding and turning within, I want you to imagine, towering above you, a great spiritual being whose presence radiates in your mind's eye. You feel an amazing power emanating from deep within this angelic presence, as waves of love wash over you.

Understand that this being is not separate, but it is another part of you, that you and this angelic being are connected, and that we want to strengthen this connection now and bring this presence closer. Closer and closer until you can begin to integrate it into your waking self.

As you breathe in, you will yourself to merge with this vision of this great spiritual being which is your higher self, and as you breathe out, you feel it entering your awareness and merging with your waking state. This being is a perfected part of you and you want to bring it closer and closer, so that as you breathe in, you feel yourself beginning to merge with this being, and as you breathe out, you feel this divine part of yourself awakening within. Breathe in and feel yourself connecting with this higher part of you breathe out you and your angelic higher self are merging into one.

As you breathe in you feel yourself becoming in tune with your higher self and as you breathe out you feel your higher self resonating within your conscious awareness.

With every inbreath strive upwards reaching out to this angelic being which is your higher self, and with every outbreath you and your higher self are becoming one. With every inbreath reach out with your heart towards this presence, and as you breathe out relax as you begin to feel these two parts of yourself coming together, so that you will be able to speak with one voice. (Pause here)

Listen carefully now in the silence and take time to receive guidance from this newly awakened part of yourself.

*Adapted from Israel Regardie's, Knowledge and Conversation with the Holy Guardian Angel. Falcon Press Recording

6. *The Lovers*

The Lovers

The appearance of an angelic being in some Tarot decks suggests that there is a part in each of us, or of the human experience at least, capable of connecting with something larger than ourselves. Depending on your religious persuasion or upbringing you may or may not have a belief in angels, but that doesn't matter here. The Sun on most Tarot archetypes represents the seat of the personality and the wholeness of being that can be achieved through inner work. Sometimes it is necessary to go through a cleansing or detoxification process several times, before you can reach the stage of initiating the conversation with ones Holy Guardian Angel. We explored that phase of purification by fire in the God of the Grove pathworking.

The figures in the Initiate's Way archetype look almost reptilian or alien and they are presenting the idea of duality, and the splitting of gender and consciousness into two distinct parts. In alchemy a sacred marriage occurs between those two parts within the imagination. The emphasis is localised to the spines of each of the figures, connecting at the heart, one has fire travelling up the spinal column and the other has a vine, or greenery growing up towards the head. They both have serpentine protrusions coming from their third eye, and in the background there is an image of the lotus wand which is about to take root in the ground, suggesting an earthing of a current that is being generated between these two beings.

Communication in all of its forms is represented in this arcana which includes otherworldly influences that we can have direct communication with, as well as our relationships with the people around us. The astrological association here is with Gemini, or the twins, and the time of year, the Summer Solstice which falls within the 21st, 22nd, and 23rd of June, when we celebrate the longest day and the shortest night. The Summer Solstice, or 'sun standing still', marks one of the four turning points in the cycle of the year. The nights begin to lengthen and the daylight gradually wanes until the next turning of the seasons at the Autumn Equinox.

You have arrived at a pivotal point in your spiritual development journey and are required to make conscious choices using the intellect, reason and logic, as opposed to intuition or gut instinct. Some decks speak of romantic love as an interpretation, and even going so far as to have a cherub pointing the arrow at a man choosing between two women. Here I am suggesting a time for a consideration of choices regarding your path in life. Do you follow in the footsteps of others, carrying on a business or tradition, and be remembered for your association with that? Or can you bring your own originality and individuality into play and leave behind a unique path?

The spiritual seeker at this stage is presented with big choices on their path. Will you choose the material, purely physical path of mundane existence or a spiritual path, with little or no regard for the materiality of fame, success and the like? Are you ready to take up the mental sword of the intellect to become a truth seeker and revealer?

Another explanation for the symbolism presented here as an allegory of a split in the psyche, or the division in the mind between left brain consciousness and right brain consciousness, with the mediating factor being the mercurial glue of the intellect which creates communication between the two states. The altered states of awareness achieved during meditation can cause one to perceive things in a very different way, than during normal waking consciousness. Performing specific meditations or brain exercises, such as these pathworkings or using hypnotherapy scripts, can initiate lasting and positive changes, purely by using the faculty of imagination.

In the instance during the pathworking that accompanies this image there is a deliberate creation of a conversation between a higher part of yourself and the part participating in the journey. There is a distinction between two very different ways of thinking, and so bringing the personality in to a balance point of union within the self by the creation of this bridge. Logic and reason or left brain thinking and the creative or intuitive right brain are dual states of awareness. One or the other usually dominates in a person until either one finally dominates over the other. Through active participation in balancing the hemispheres there can be an integration of the third aspect of self or the accessing of the higher self, who mediates between these after being introduced into the personality. When someone says they are talking to god it may be that they have initiated this process naturally.

In alchemy this is the process of bringing together the solar and lunar aspects of the personality with mercurius as the glue ie, Solve et coagula.

Numerologically you could look at this archetype as choosing between different traditions. The sixth Sephiroth on the Tree of life is concerned with harmony, beauty, and religious function. Even though Religion and spirituality are two very different things and you may find yourself discovering some traditional roots within your own family lines and ancestral heritage, which will always be a part of who you are. Though it is your choice whether or not to carry on along the same path. You may want to break

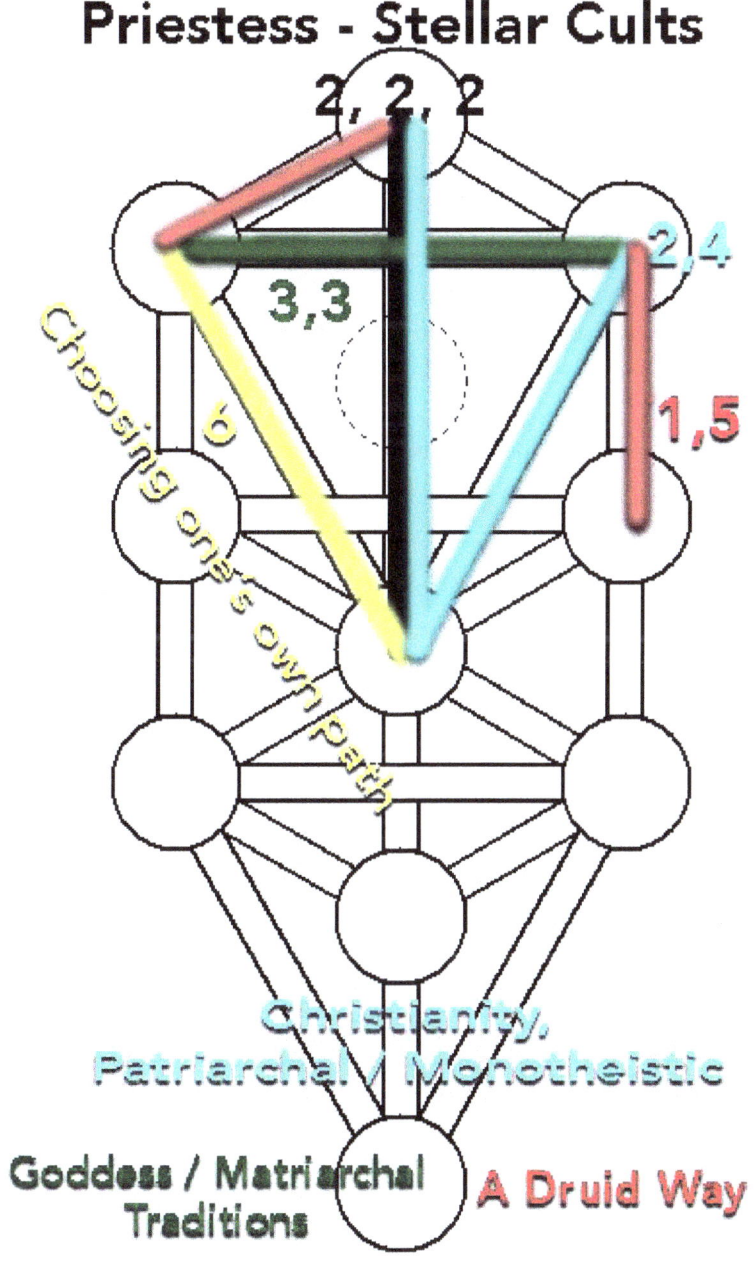

away from the familial beliefs and go with something that feels more in line with who you truly are. There is always a choice.

1, 5 A Druid Way?
2, 4 Christianity, patriarchal or other monotheistic belief?
2, 2, 2 Priestess or stellar cults?
3, 3 Goddess or matriarchal traditions?
6 Choosing a path of your own!

If you consider the number six as a harmonic perspective from the centre of your being, having reached this centre or still point, you can begin to hear your inner voice, listen to your own guidance and the teachings that you have been trying to give yourself in the silence and stillness of contemplation in meditation.

Initiating conversation with your higher self, or holy guardian angel. The way forward from here is perfecting ones self, seeing beauty in the world, living in harmony and balancing of opposites. A re-alignment and re-connection with the divine nature and the awakening of the individual star that you are.

On one level you are dealing with the idea of your higher self, or guardian angel. Whatever you call that aspect of yourself that will forever strive towards acting for the greater good of all and not for purely selfish motives. On the other level, the aspirations and ideals of those with particular beliefs, who act according to what they think is in the best interests of others within the constraints of their belief system. Humanitarian thinking, charity, tolerance and kindness towards others are often the fundamental ideals promoted within religious frameworks and are all personality traits worth nurturing in our selves and others.

Exercise

Draw an image of two triangles one pointing downwards and one pointing upwards, side by side. If you imagine that the downward pointing triangle represents the part of yourself that you are bringing into consciousness during the pathworking meditation,. The upwards pointing triangle is the waking state of awareness that you are in right now, which aspires towards this union, next to it draw a six pointed star by drawing the upwards pointing triangle on top of the downwards triangle, to produce a star of David, it then becomes one entity.

Symbolically this is what we are trying to achieve as we bring this new state of awareness into being, which in turn then expands our conscious awareness outside of its normal waking state.

The enlightenment journey is cyclical and I again refer you to the idea presented by R.J Stewart concerning the three faces of Merlin, in his book *The Prophetic Vision of Merlin,* about the three fates or goddess transitions. The combination of the three fates and the three faces of Merlin suggests a lineage or tradition in which the feminine and masculine mysteries play an active part.

Everyone comes to this life with a unique set of circumstances and perhaps in time you may discover a hereditary line of ancestral beliefs or worship of those who went before you. In that succession or line of generation you literally become the torch bearer of life, as it passes from one generation to the next. So the beliefs, memories, and experiences of those who have gone before, are there and accessible in an ancestral pool. You also have a choice whether or not to become a distillery in the human alchemical processes, and as you prepare to die to the old parts of yourself, and imbibe the past, so that you can move into your self created future, looking through a newly created spiritual lens.

Manly Palmer Hall suggests that the traditional Lovers image represents the youth choosing to willingly go into a life of maturity, a path of virtue, and that the image of fate had been mistakenly ascribed to cupid. If the youth happens to choose vice instead of virtue, one can imagine the outcome of that scenario.

It may not always be a bed of roses to activate one's free will and there may also be a heavy price to pay, but it is a decision between enslavement or freedom from the entrapments of the mind. With choice comes responsibility.

Questions

Are you ready to become a torch bearer? Are your thoughts and ideas a product of who you are or an after effect of social conditioning and peer pressure? Who or what lies in your heart and mind? Where are you in terms of your own spiritual cycle? Would you say you at the beginning of birthing as a new being, or innocent child, or are you more like the wisened one able to look at your own mistakes and those of others with compassion and kindness?

Chariot of the Moon

Inhale deeply and let your breath out slowly. Begin your journey inward and begin breathing in 2,3,4 and out 2,3,4. The noises and the distractions of the outside world begin to fade away as you move deeper and deeper within your self. As you become more and more relaxed you notice that you are not in fact standing still. There is a strong sensation of movement. Go deeper still and focus your attention on this movement. Your inner core feels like it has an impenetrable shell like an armadillo's armour to protect itself and you may have to break through these layers to get through.

As you travel within and begin moving through the layers of protection that you have built around yourself you become aware of a veil of fine indigo mist coming towards you. The mist envelopes your vision.

The swirling indigo colour you see brings a sense of peaceful, tranquil serenity which washes through you in waves of ecstatic bliss. The closer you get to your centre the more peaceful and serene you become. The indigo begins to change colour into a deep midnight blue and you perceive an opening in the mist.

I want you to imagine a cave entrance, forming in front of you. You feel drawn towards this cave, eager to encounter this secret place. Feel your ancestors and the presence of the gods and goddesses drawing near. I want you to reach into this cave entrance with your full awareness and immerse yourself totally in the experience. The darkness is alive, comforting and pregnant with possibilities. You are entering into a different time and place, a secret world. For a moment you can't see anything but you can feel the tunnel ahead of you and I want you to begin to will yourself forward through the darkness.

(Short pause.)

Now you can see a speck of light a little way ahead in the distance, only a tiny glow at first but as you travel towards it you recognise it as the face of the gleaming moon in the darkness. As you get closer to the moon you leave the tunnel behind you now. You find yourself outside in a starlit landscape. A midnight sky above you and a rocky ground underneath your feet. The moonbeams illuminate a carriage that has been waiting here for you. Its presence is bright and you connect with a strong energy coming from the chariot which you recognise as being the pulse that also radiates from within your being. You climb into your chariot and the force of the lunar tide pulls at your body. Experience the flux.

Four magnificent creatures are bridled to your vehicle and they awaken to your silent call. The rocks gleam with rainbow hues and as your chariot moves along this shining path you travel towards the bright full moon. Your senses are keen and alive and as the chariot moves forward it lifts off the ground. You are almost at the moon and as you travel into the light of the moon you feel a part of your self ascending, evolving and changing. You leave behind you any doubt or fears that may have held you back. Your power is being restored. This is your time to shine.

Spend a few moments basking in the essence of everything that is you. This is the core of you and you can come back to this place anytime you need to recharge and replenish your lost energies, confidence or self esteem.

7. *The Chariot of the Moon*

Chariot of the Moon

You are looking at a warrior here who is poised and ready to charge but where is this going to lead? Traditionally on some Tarot decks you see two black and white horses or sphinx drawing the cart. On the Initiate's Way image the chariot is being drawn by four horses or individual 'powers' of constant creation, which reside within each individual, the synthesis of which is an awakened hidden power which can be tapped into at any time, so that you may descend into the underworld, fearless, and unafraid of what you may find.

Manly Palmer Hall in his *Secret Teachings of all Ages* talks about the seven planets being the chariots that contain and harness solar power. The four 'powers' are the 'mighty ones' that you can perhaps understand as the archangels. Four horses that signify the coming of an apocalypse (revealing and awakening), or the four streams of wisdom that are accessible through the vehicle of the chariot. That is to say that once the body of light has been constructed and the seeker travels in it to higher levels of awareness, they can then gain access to information that they would not normally be able to reach due to only functioning in the lower levels associated with the three lower chakras or energy centres.

This process of ascension is a personal thing and the experience is an internal one. There is certainly an idea of regeneration being presented here and the arrow that is being aimed directly at the moon is showing you, that the journey ahead will take you through the underworld to explore the realm of the shadows.

Going willingly in to the underworld at the sign of cancer around the time of the summer solstice and returning to the light at the other end of the procession of the equinoxes at the winter solstice. What is most important here is the idea of movement, getting into the driving seat of your life and gaining self mastery. If you understand the solar aspect of personality as being awake or switched on and the lunar aspect of consciousness as that which is unconscious. You can choose to flick a switch in your consciousness and remain awake, realising that the information contained within the unconscious is accessible to you, once you find a way to reach this information through meditation and ritual.

A chariot would have served many purposes in the past, one of which was a weapon or an instrument of war and as an iconic representation of royal power or heroic symbolism. On one level this image represents conflict, that may mean a fight where one needs to be self assertive, however we usually find that it is more likely suggestive of getting ourselves into a stronger position to be able to manifest successful outcomes to our problems. Think about self control and the use of one's willpower.

The power of words and especially the spoken word are important concepts to consider here. Discovering your innate abilities, key skills and being able to articulate your needs, wants and desires to others in the form of words in an assertive but not a domineering way.

Self reliance and reaching a point of union within yourself enables you as the seeker to form a light body, or a vehicle of ascension. You can then get into the spiritual realm and travel easily in and out of mystical states of awareness, where you can transmit and receive information. The terminology may be different depending on your discipline but mystical states, waking dreams, out of body experiences and dreamwalking on the astral plane, all fall into the category of experiences to expect at this stage of the journey.

Once you begin to understand the different modes of awareness that you move through, and have control over them to be able to switch them on and off at will. You are then gaining more understanding of the immense capacity for growth contained within your awareness as a human being, which in turn gives you more self control. When you look into the deeper meaning of the split psyche suggested in the previous card, here you will find an integration of those opposing parts resulting in a greater understanding of higher levels of awareness.

The opposing states of war and peace that you have within, can now be brought into equilibrium as you begin to manage yourself, via controlling your emotions and any reactions that you may have to situations and events in the exoteric world. All of a sudden it is as if the mist rolls away from your eyes as hidden senses are awakened within. You then become the conquerer and the corrector of imbalances from a place of stability, and a focussed centre, to be able to see things differently than you did before. Consciousness transcends out of ordinary awareness and functions on lots of different levels simultaneously.

When this image turns up in a reading it is the driving force within each individual which is their storehouse of potential energy, and once it has been tapped into, it then becomes an endless power source for further development. One of the names for this image is the Chariot of the Moon, the mythological idea represents is a personification of the Moon or a lunar deity, specifically the full moon aspect of the lunar triple goddesses, she drives a chariot drawn by horses or oxen and has a male counterpart in one of the solar deities who ride in their Chariots of the Sun.

A chariot drawn by oxen can be understood as the third aspect of the triple goddess, that of the crone. She carries away the souls of the dead, with one of her names being Hecate and it is she who stands at the doorway presiding over the death and rebirth process as the Goddess of Crossroads. This archetype can also be associated with agriculture and the division of land for the purposes of farming, and also on another level with the idea of a mighty warrior riding into battle on a chariot which is drawn by animals and more often than not battling over ownership of land. The Egyptian connection that we see on some versions of this image begs you to understand the riddle of the Sphinx. Also your inner and outer worlds, the male and female aspects of the personality are engaging with a newly awakened awareness. This will help you to complete a stage in the enlightenment process, and to move on or ascend into a different way of perceiving. The black and the white sphinxes sit between the worlds of waking awareness and the realm of the dreaming, meaning the dark and light. Understanding the effect that hidden or subconscious content has on our waking awareness can bring about balance within the psyche.

The *Conqueror* is not asking you to conquer other people but to be aware of your true motivations when dealing with others. Asking will you use your wisdom and knowledge to assist others on their path or will you fall in to the trap of using it to subjugate others to your will? In Egypt temples of the past rose and fell, some into obscurity, others changed and evolved and grew anew depending on the nature of those who were creating and worshipping in them. The four elements are also worth a consideration here, our connection with them on an emotional level and to a certain extent our affinity with them, which will determine our personality traits.

For example if you are by nature someone who is sensitive to the feelings of others and very receptive to the external environment, we would say that the person has a watery personality. Likewise someone who is very cerebral and spends a lot of time thinking, we would say they are an airy type of personality.

The division of personality archetypes into the signs of the zodiac offers a journey in itself as a process of working through each of these archetypes. Beginning with Aries in April, Taurus in May, Gemini in June and so on until you have worked through the cycle. By becoming aware on the inner plane of each part of the personality types represented by the zodiac, we can align with each and perform a cleansing or clearing out, of any psychic junk that we have accrued within our consciousness. Jung talks about this process in Psychology and Alchemy:

> In the Manichean system the saviour constructs a cosmic wheel with twelve buckets – the zodiac – for the raising of souls. The wheel has a significant connection with the rota or opus circulatorium of alchemy, which serves the same purpose of sublimation. As Dorn says: "The wheel of creation takes its rise from the prima materia whence it passes to the simple elements." Ripley says: "The wheel must be turned by the four seasons and the four quarters thus connecting the symbol with the peregrinatio (Journey/Pilgrimage) and the quaternity (group or a set of four). The wheel turns into the wheel

of the sun rolling around the heavens, and so becomes identical with the sun-god or hero who submits to arduous labours and to the passage of self cremation, like herakles, or to captivity like Osiris. A well known parallel to the chariot of the sun is the fiery chariot on which Elijah ascended to heaven.

– Carl Jung *Psychology and Alchemy* pp380-1)

This would suggest that in a year there is the potential for one full turning of a karmic wheel beginning in April and ending in March the following year, with the awakening and aligning of each of the twelve zodiac signs in turn. Then attuning to each particular archetype during meditation in a cyclical process, so that the cycle repeats like the journey of the sun and the moon during each procession of the equinox.

On a personal level you are being asked to look at the emotional aspect of your life, the fulfilled or unfulfilled dreams that you have, what you secretly desire and whether or not reality lives up to your hopes, dreams and expectations.

You are at a point in the journey of self-realization where you can understand your true nature by overcoming the false or projected persona, and gaining insight into the laws of nature and your part within it. The association with the moon makes it a time to pay more attention to cycles and transitions, your home, where you live, your family and your commitments in life and whether they are in harmony with your inner world. You can look to the stars and the myths for insight and deeper meaning and when reading for people remember that the timescale denoted here is that of early summertime.

Numerologically you can also look at this image as 1 1 1 1 1 1 1 being a synthesis of the seven different archetypes that we have covered so far in the text. Each image up until this one can be understood as an archetype, but this is the first stereotypical image of the questing hero/heroine entering the underworld. At the beginning of the journey the Fool stepped onto the path and made the decision to become a Magi or one who controls their own destiny. After travelling inward and experiencing the God and Goddess within, meeting and receiving guidance from the inner teacher then began the process of self refinement at the Lovers image. So now you understand that to become your true potential you must create yourself anew. The Chariot is the vehicle in which you do this, you begin with your physical body as your temple and then learn to treat it with respect, listening to your body's consciousness. To take in what it is trying to tell you and when you should change something in order to perfect your vehicle for transition. This may at some point involve initiation into one of the healing systems or learning of the old ways, or even rediscovering lost ways.

If you think of each archetype that has gone before as different aspects of the personality within and in the greater perspective as seven different traditions or lineages from the past which still have an influence on you today.

Exercise:

1 & 6. Take out the Messenger/Magician from a Tarot deck and place it above the Lovers and think of the information we have discussed in the last chapter. Through the application of ritual and magic using willpower, love and the full faculties of our

consciousness. We can instigate change and movement, directing influence and creating our vehicle for moving onward and upwards, figuratively and literally.

One of the names for this process is the Merkaba; "Mer" meaning light, "Ka" representing spirit and "Ba" meaning body. You are literally creating a light body in which you can travel to other realms to receive wisdom, teachings and information that you would not otherwise be able to reach in normal waking states of consciousness. It is often referred to as a vehicle for teachings to be transmitted back and forth through time. The activation of the spirit body or light body is the process of ascension and a creation of your own light and spirit body, or chariot. The term Chakra translates roughly as spinning wheel and when all of your Chakras/energy centres are all functioning in harmony with each other, you can reach the perfect union with yourself and the universe. This will lead to you to being open to the receiving and transmitting of your own frequency, as well as channeling the information from the teachers who went before us. The idea being that ascended masters use these spinning vortices when working with those still here on the earth plane, and in receiving attunements in the various energy healing systems you can access this vibrational frequency and *tune in* to those who went before you.

Exercise:

2,5. Take out the High Priestess and the Heirophant/Shaman Tarot cards and ponder any significance or relationship that you perceive between these two Archetypes. *Keywords*: Perfection. Attainment. Openness. Receiving. Cleansing. Refinement.

Questions:

Are you ready to cleanse your body, mind, soul, and spirit? Are there areas in your life that have accumulated clutter? (This can mean physical hoarding as well as emotional baggage, spiritual dead weight or beliefs that no longer serve, and stagnant ways of thinking that require cleansing.)

Meditation for Strength by Caitlín Matthews

Breathe and be still. Be aware of the sky above, the land below and the four directions that surround you. Now from each of these six points a shooting star comes running – from above, below, and from on all four sides of you – meeting in the centre, over your heart, opening a door within.

Step into the doorway that they have opened. Trust that all that you experience within, whether from your sight, smell, hearing, taste or feeling, will be discerned and remembered in the cells of your body.

You stand in an atrium, a small hallway, from which lead two doors. In the centre, between these doors is a shrine on which stands the statue of a Lion with an open mouth. Whatever your issue or question at this time, come now and lay it inside the mouth of the Lion. Trust that you will understand more when you return.

Taking the left hand doorway, pass within and ascend the steep, curving, silver stairs that meet you. Climb them to the top, where you emerge upon a platform that looks upon the great vast beauty of the night sky. One star is calling you and you want to rise higher. With all your heart, call upon the Shepherd of Souls to send you a way of going there.

No sooner have you conceived this desire than a beast comes padding down to where you wait. If you have the body of the man, then the beast is a lioness; if you have the body of the woman, then the beast is a lion. You are invited to ride upon the back of the beast, holding onto the red reins that lie lightly about its neck.

The beast rises towards the star that you have desired to visit. You pass through the heavens towards the star and land upon it, in a land that is familiar to you. Here is a tall waterfall spilling into a wide pool, making a beautiful music. As the spray arcs, its drops fall upon you and unto the lion or lioness. Look into the waters. Within reach there is an object or symbol. Take it forth. As you touch it, what happens? What do you experience?

As you show it to the beast beside you, how does it react to this object and to you as its bearer? Behold yourself in the beast's eyes, as it bows to you. You may bow back in acknowledgement of the gift that you each have within you. Neither of you is better or worse, higher or lower than the other: you are both together, of equal worth and strength.

From within the depths of the waterfall, a spiritual being shows itself to you: the Shepherd of Souls is present and blesses you and the beast. Feel how the strength within you and the beast are enhanced as you are overshadowed briefly by it passing through you. Know and remember that feeling.

This is a place to which you can always return.

The beast stirs and bids you mount upon its back again. You leave the place of the waterfall, departing from the star as the lion or lioness pads through the night sky and brings you to a platform, this time at the top of the golden stairs.

You and the beast press forehead to forehead, and mingle your breath, bidding farewell for this time.

Pass down the steeply curving golden stairs, emerging into the atrium through the other door from the one you ascended. Now you go to the Shrine of the Lion where you left your issue or question. With the object that you brought back from the star in one hand, take your issue out of the lion's mouth. *What do you understand now that you didn't before? What has changed? What is possible?*

Whatever the original shape or nature of the object you took from the pool, now it shines in your hand like a star. Hold to your star and place it within your body safely.

The high calling of shooting stars rings in your ears and you emerge from the temple of your heart. The sky is above, the land below. The four directions are on each side of you. Open your eyes and hold to your star: the strength of the gift that lives inside you.

8. *Strength / Fortitude*

Strength / Fortitude

This archetype suggests the duality of human nature and animal instincts. You see the face of a great goddess and a lion/ess merging together as one and underneath there is a symbol that keeps recurring. I have taken this to represent the opening of a door/doors through which there is a flow of information and wisdom that can be switched on and off using that symbol. I painted this strength/fortitude image during August 2017 at the same time as taking a priestess atunement with the Fellowship of Isis. For me this image will always represent the coming together with others collectively on a path.

On several versions of this image in the Tarot we find a lady with a lion and there is a great deal of controversy over whether she is opening or closing the mouth of the lion. It appears to me that she is showing her fearlessness by opening the lion's mouth as a gesture of mutual trust. Symbolically you can take this as representing the stage in the spiritual journey where you have found the elusive hidden strength within, a spiritual strength that everyone has inside. You can now begin to act from that place of inner strength that was previously unobtainable. Becoming attuned with the mysteries and wisdom of the past will give you a much broader perspective from which to tread your unique path.

Consider the astrological sign of Leo the lion, which is also attributed to this image. Also consider those ancestors who once gazed upon the constellation of Leo, coming from a different time but awaiting the rediscovery of their secrets and wisdom.

The lemniscate or infinity symbol that appears in this image features above the head of the Magician and indicates a continuity of wisdom that has no end. It also suggests the cyclical motion and the repetition of that cycle. Coming back to the present moment each time after going into the past and looking to the future, realising that the only place you can make real change is in the present moment now.

Strength/Fortitude By Caitlín Matthews

The Ancient Egyptians believed that, when human beings entered the afterlife, the final state of the human soul was as an imperishable star that would shine forever in the firmament. When we look up into the night sky, it is easy to understand that: a myriad constellations, millions upon millions of stars, each having their own place in the universe.

For us, the challenge of Strength is to find the trajectory of our own potential for, within each person, lie a thousand doorways to stars uncounted, doorways that we seldom access. Over each of our heads shines a special light that is descriptive of our personal array of gifts and aptitudes: gifts that were woven into our being from ancestors and spiritual beings who have imbued our nature with distinct potentials. Everyone who meets us can see this light more clearly than we ourselves: knowing or feeling what gifts that light bestows upon us, they can ask us for help, service, or advice.

Strength enables us to know ourselves and our potential, to open those long-shut doors into our soul. When we go within, we suddenly access a power we never imagined could manifest through our words, deeds and thoughts.

Sadly that potential that lies within each of us often goes unused, ignored, untapped. Rather than using it and accessing it with passion, we sometimes underestimate what we are capable of, or else mistakenly try to save our potential for a mythical rainy day, therefore missing the opportunity for our light to shine. It is often fear and lack of confidence that blocks the way, or the unthinking words of people who have judged us that we have believed.

Fear of our smallness, unworthiness or lack of skill can keep us likewise weak and small. Strength is just one side of the coin: flick the coin downwards and fear is face-up, locking power face-down, unaccessed. But flick the coin upwards and fear is locked down.

If the gift that you were born to deliver lies still within you, unexpressed, then it is time to waken your soul and go on a quest for the shepherd of your soul – the spiritual being that holds you dear and who knows the path that your tread. The strength that we gain when our spirit guides accompany and support us, enables us not only to draw upon our own potential, but to enhance and share theirs too. By this miraculous cooperation we turn our fear into a power that springs up glorious in its service, a strength that helps the whole world.

Questions

Who are you? Where does your strength lie? Where can you use your strengths? How can you balance power with love, and lovingly express your power? How do you harness your desires or harness your rages? What powers lie untapped in you? What are you wrestling with? What gift is striving to be expressed from your depths? Where is your gift needed now?

Merlin The Hermit – Son of the Mother

Begin breathing in and breathe out to the count of four. With every breath you feel more and more relaxed. When you breathe in, push your stomach out and when you breathe out, let it fall naturally. Repeat this process until you are completely relaxed, open and receptive. I want you to imagine that you are walking along a densely populated forest path.

You are surrounded by tall oak trees interspersed with holly at their roots. As you walk along this old track you feel comfortable and safe. The many hues of green around you tug at your heart and you feel the gentle touch of nature's breath against your skin. Look down at your feet and study the path directly beneath you. What do you see on the ground under your feet? Feel the gentle breeze as it whispers through the leaves. Sunlight breaks in beams through the leaves and spills onto the forest floor.

Keep walking along the path further into the heart of this sacred woodland. You hear rustling in the foliage just off to your right and you turn your attention towards it. Peeking out from behind a bush there is a fawn. She smells the air and sensing no fear she looks directly at you. Just for one moment you are captivated by the beauty of this creature, then something startles her and she darts away back into the undergrowth. A wave of serenity washes over you as you have been lucky enough to share a moment with the beautiful fawn.

Up ahead you notice an opening in the trees and you make your way towards it. You feel drawn to this part of the forest and eager to see what you will discover.

As you walk through the opening in the trees you are presented with a glorious sight. An open clearing with a stone labyrinth on the floor. The sun beams down on the pattern and you know you have to walk this now. You feel like you have done this a long time ago and as you begin to tread the path as so many before you have done, your awareness of the outside world begins to ebb away as you spiral in towards the centre of the pattern. You see yourself walking to the centre of the labyrinth and as you stand there it feels as though you have begun to grow roots. These roots extend far down into the *earth seeking connection with the goddess, Gaia herself, our mother. Pause here.*

You stand in the middle of the labyrinth, you begin to realise your purpose. You are joined now by a companion. Slowly it begins to dawn on you why you came here seeking. You already know who you are. Spend a moment here in your centre as you remember and allow the images to come.

Long pause before carrying on.

You are open and ready to receive. Take a deep breath and ready yourself. You are going to take with you everything that you sensed, felt, thought or saw, as you walk back out of the labyrinth the way you came and slowly return to your normal waking state.

Take your time walking back along the path, winding in and out of the corners and back to the entrance where you began. You feel alive, excited, calm and serene. You can come back to this place anytime you need to be at one with yourself and the world around you.

The forest path awaits you and this time you walk through it with a lightness in your stride as if you are literally walking on air. Being on your own and at peace with yourself gives you the courage to start making changes in your life. As you walk back along the forest path, consider the immediate things that require attention.

The time is now and now it is time to be your own guide.

When you feel ready open your eyes and have a drink of water and record your experiences in your journal. If you are working in a group take some time to discuss your experiences and learn from each other.

9. Merlin The Hermit – Son of the Mother

Merlin The Hermit – Son of the Mother

In Tarot usually you will find here a male figure of the wise old man archetype which I attribute to Merlin. The importance of silence and retreat from the physical world for the purpose of meditation is stressed here, and the internal seeking of one's own being. In terms of psychology this archetype represents a journey into the underworld or the world of shadows. If you cast a light onto something, it casts a shadow and you cannot ignore it, instead you must retreat further into the silence and reintegrate these parts of yourself before you can progress any further on this journey. In silence, solitude and retreat is where you can heal yourself, by going within and spending time alone. It is an intensely personal journey and each person is unique by having different life circumstances, but if you do not allow yourself significant time to explore the shadows and avoid doing inner work on yourself, it can manifest in physical and mental illness. The hermit is carrying a staff which is topped with the orphic egg, also being protected by the snake that is climbing up the staff, this is a universal symbol for wisdom.

In the cycle of the year as the sun moves out of Virgo and into Libra in October, autumn begins and it is the time for beginning to break down the old to make way for the new. The "leaves" or outmoded thoughts, perceptions or beliefs fall away as you go headlong into the darkness and introspection of winter. Darker nights and cold weather mean retreating to the hearthside with those you love and concentrating on strengthening family bonds. This image of the hermit is a personification of seeking innate and ancestral wisdom.

This is the lonely old hermit, psychopomp, guide or teacher who can help you to navigate the dark places within your own soul. For if you do not confront all of your shadows then how are you to become wise?

Manly Palmer Hall in his *Secret Teachings of the Ages* talks about this figure being a guardian of the light of ancient wisdom. One who protects it from falling into the hands of the wrong kinds of people and thereby suggests that he is the embodiment of the secret organisations who hide this light from the profane. His staff is his support and the foundation upon which the knowledge rests. The idea of the human body as a temple, once it is recognised as such, is a good subject for meditation here. By retreating within and becoming stable on your own foundations you allow progression and inner work to be the catalyst to lasting changes to your personality.

Questions

Are you giving yourself enough time for reflection? Are you ready to perform spiritual alchemy on yourself and shed those things that no longer serve you? Are you comfortable in your own company or are there things that require inner work before you can progress along the path?

Primal Numbers, on the Path of the Hermit By Richard Abbot

At first glance the esoteric world of souls bears little relevance to the world of numbers and the arithmetic of 1+1=2 seems stagnant besides the awesomeness of light and shadow. Yet each interleaves with the other for all things magickal contain the silver thread of numbers. To pull on the end of this thread is not to enter into a bookkeeping flatland, but to begin a trail involving cosmic forces of the highest order.

Numbers Are Everywhere. Numbers are often mistakenly viewed as some man-made abstract, or worse still, as an impediment to the flow of love, light and truth. But none of this is true once we recognise that numbers are stitched into every spiritual and occult practice under the sun from the 4 elements of the Magus, to the 7 rays of the Theosophists, the 64 hexagrams of the I Ching, the Wiccan law of 3-fold return and the 78 cards of the Tarot. This is because the very essence of the worlds around us – visible and invisible – is numerical. We are not talking here of the ever-presence of the clock or the calendar, but of the very things that construct humanity; the four fingers of the hand, the one thumb, the two arms, the five orifices of the head (ears, nostrils and mouth), the two breasts and the one phallus. The primal nature of all things human can be understood by their numbers.

For example: 22 – the total number of Major Arcana – is considered sacred due to its intimacy with the human body. What makes humans unique from all other species alive on the planet? They have 8 fingers, 2 thumbs and 10 toes.

That's 20 useful tools. They also have a tongue with which to speak (21) and, depending on gender, 1 generative organ. That's a magickal 22. Another number all humans embody is 3. Each man has 2 testicles and 1 penis, while each woman has 1 vagina and 2 ovaries. Applying the formula $3 + 3 = 6$ we reveal The Lovers VI, the card of love and union, where the creative 3's work together to co-create. The Hermit understands formulae such as this, and applies them in all his works.

Numbers Generate Life

The Hermit is also aware that one of the laws of Planet Earth is limitation. Humans have at their disposal a limited number of days in one lifetime.

Few may know this number, but all know that in the physical form their days are finite. Though there are many other limitations, natural or artificial, this is the one with which all humans must grapple. Through limitation pressure is exerted, and tension and compression generated in daily human life. Though some may display a New Age immaturity toward this fact and indeed seek to deny or negate it, others might recognise the magnificent gift that is bestowed, for tension and limitation allows the construction of the altar upon which a human life may be dedicated. Upon this altar of limitation there may be performed occult rituals of initiation, or there simply be the fresh urgency of each new day under the prime force of the 1, the rising Sun (Card 19 = 10 =1).

Under these conditions the manner in which each individual works with limitation will always vary, but the truth is apparent – that creation is formed from the pressure of the finite, as shown by/ number; and that the limitless is only ever born from the limited, with necessity as the cosmic mother of invention. This primal urge to create (as well as its polar opposite, to destroy) is the basis of all numbers, for the story of numbers is the desire of 'nothing' to become 'something', the unmanifest to manifest and the invisible to become visible.

First there was nothing – 0. It had no tendency or inclination in any direction whatsoever. It wanted to do nothing and be nothing. In fact it didn't even want to do that, for to name something as nothing is to call it something! This was a different type of nothingness that extended outside any arrangement, system, language or law. Then, one day, there was something. It was the number 1. This spark appeared at the behest of the cosmic instruction 'Let There Be Light'.

And even though there immediately was Light, the 1 quickly discovered that it really was the loneliest number, to such an extent that it could not remain as 1 a moment longer. Once called into being the 1 desired to grow and the only way it could do that was through self-knowledge, which came through relief – the casting of Light upon it-self in order to reveal it's not-self. After all, how can anything ever be known other than by comparison? And so, as night follows day, the 2 was born. Now the Light of Fire and its opposite in 2, the darkness of Water, set about balancing and adjusting the world around them. They soon discovered that they needed to stay apart from one another and mix only in certain circumstances.

The 3 was born from this process, itself containing all the things that the 1 and 2 were, as well as what they were not. This 3 took the form of Air and acted as the intermediary between the actions of the primal elements Fire (1) and Water (2).

At this point we can see that although this is the story of all creation, it is also the story of daily human existence with its projects, efforts, interactions and endeavors. First they don't exist (0), and then suddenly a spark flashes (1). This grows; quickly reaching out from what it might be to what it might not be (2). Its possible success is counterbalanced by its possible failure, its creation by its destruction, its reward by its cost. This duality is the Realm of the 2, the place of dilemma, the anxiety of like/dislike and procrastination of yes/no. Many humans can initiate and originate (1), but many others cannot get beyond the stage of the 2, particularly those of a Watery nature. The Hermit knows this yet welcomes all. When the realisation is reached by the 2 that the answer to all questions is AND, not OR then balance is achieved.

This brings forth the Zone of the 3 where all things can be assimilated and conjoined in a creative triangle within which the 1 sacrifices a part of itself in order to become 2 and in turn the 2 releases part of its energy in order to become 3. And yet the process is still not complete for once the 3 has stabilized so it must give forth a primal scream, such that a new and independent life is manifested at its centre. This is the number 4, the primal force of Earth, which though an element in its own right is also the element that contains all the other elements.

All this is explained and resolved in the Hermetic Formula of Creation:

$$1+2+3+4 = 10$$
$$1+0 = 1$$

This primal fourness – Fire, Water, Air and Earth, seen in all things high and low and intrinsic to a functioning life – brings forth a new spark of Fire in its resultant 1 and the cycle of Life rolls on, played out in the Tarot through the lenses of the four court cards and the four suits.

It is possible to apply these primal principles in daily life in quite practical ways.

0 shows that nothing always begets something. Because nature abhors a vacuum daily tasks will always take up as much time as we have available, showing us, maybe, that are days will somehow always be full no matter what we have to do.

1 points to the uniqueness that is each individual human life, while 2 reflects the need of that individual for challenging, as well as harmonious, encounters with other unique individuals. Many people do not enjoy this dual aspect of life, yet the numbers prove that trying to avoid it is literally like trying to avoid ever getting wet. It can't be done.

3 brings the synthesis to the opposition, the offspring of the parents, the products of the disagreement and love of the opposing 2. Even the most incandescent ideas and brightest individuals have to compromise, adapt and give a little in order to get what they need. Purity exists only in the Fiery 1, yet that Fire itself desires to be extinguished, such that its power may be distributed elsewhere. Without the balance of Water (2) the burning Fire is no longer creative, but destructive. This is the long story of the Wand and the Cup, the male and female and the varying (im)balances of the sexes.

4 then connects into the manifest world all around. This is the primal world recognized by the original Hermit, the sorcerer Merlin, who cried in the days of his greatest despair "why is it that the seasons are not all the same?" Though he was railing against the fourness of the sun, wind, rain and snow his lament may now be updated to "why aren't people all the same, why can they not all agree?"

The Hermit's answer is shown in that same Formula of Creation 1+2+3+4=10.

The nature of an individual life (1) is to encounter both harmony and conflict (2), in order to create (3) something independent and manifest (4). To take one step on this trail is to inevitably reach the end. To connect with the primal elements of the present world is to plant the seeds of a new one.

The Hermit also takes these laws and applies them to his own path. He takes great strides in order to know himself (1) then armed with that equipment sets to battle with his darker self (2). This inner war may rage for years, or even decades of human time, yet is concluded in a flash of cosmic time, and from this battle and truce is born the Hermit's unique creation, his truth (3 – Air) which he then speaks to those who ask. The next step is for the Hermit's words to form their own independent reality, made manifest beyond him, built to outlast him. All this may take one, or more lifetimes, yet so long as the Hermit continues he will be also to draw strength from the rich and lustrous material stitched into the inner lining of his rough outer cloak. The fact that no-one sees how supported and cared for he really is forms part of his strength.

Autumn by Jade Melany

Darkness descends with the rain
It's that time of year again
Retreat within and stay close to the fire
Friends and family gather together
Breathe in the magic that haunts the air
As our ancestors draw near

Sing songs in remembrance
Of those who walked before us
Give thanks for 'Life' they gave us
For they are the blessed ones
Those spirit lights we perceive
As veils thin to the other side
Open your heart and your circle wide
Reach out to them inside
As the nights draw in
And the moon grows larger
Take a moment to ponder
Reflect upon actions this year
What would you change?
Or could have done better?
Make amends or bring back to balance?
Start again with renewed vigour
Let go of outmoded thoughts

Beliefs, or things that help you not
Judge nothing but your own actions
And bring peace into your Heart.

23rd Oct 2010

Hermit by Jade Melany

Awakened serpent within the mound
Treasures once lost, now found
The voice speaks from within
Hello old friend here we are again
Singing long forgotten songs
Travelling byways
Following ancient paths
Together at last
Mind meets body
Soul entwined

Inner journeying through time
Past, present, future meld
Together into one shell

I hear the music in the distance
The pipes of Pan/Hermes
I follow the footsteps
As he leads his merry way
Dancing through the forest
With Flora, Fauna and Fae
Moving with rhythm
Charming the snakes
I heard a voice calling my name
In the old oak grove
As I sat in the circle
Of the old grey stones
The wise one came to bestow

Gifts of prophecy and wisdom
And knowledge of the trees:

Merlin, wild man of the woods
Merlin, the sorcerer misunderstood
Merlin, the magician who waves his wand
Merlin, the fool steps out once more

I heard the sound of hooves on the ground
Fleeting glance of a creature I beheld
Bestowed upon me grace and healing
Basking in sunlight
In a deserted druids grove
I feel alive once more

Acceptance into the circle of Those;

Who walked this earth before us
Who guard the Sacred Groves
Whose powers are limitless
Whose strength is untold

You have my word, my honour and my faith
Thank you Hermit (Merlin) for showing me the way

1st Sept 2017

Wheel of Fortune

Breathe deeply and get yourself into a calm relaxed state of awareness before we begin. With every breath out you feel more and more relaxed. Begin to count in and out to the steady count of four.

Focus your attention and awareness for a moment on your brain and your thoughts. Imagine that the synapses between the two hemispheres of your brain are glowing and fusing new pathways, as you attain a calm state of heightened awareness and serene relaxation.

It is dark in the temple of your mind in the midst of the deep blue of a starry night. You perceive yourself standing up on top of a green hill contemplating a beautiful skyscape of twinkling stars above you. Just for a second you sense the movement of the earth as it rotates with you standing upon it.

The image of you begins to grow taller and expands, meanwhile the earth appears to shrink underneath your feet, until you are left standing on a round ball with the galaxies spinning around your head.

In turn you see four creatures. A Man, an Eagle, a Lion and a Bull. Remember their characteristics and anything that they have to say to you.

Pause a little while here.

A shape begins to materialize in front of you. It is a spinning golden ring and as you focus your attention on it, you become aware of its eight spokes in the centre.

Which direction is your wheel spinning?

Sparks of light and lightening bolts begin to shoot out from inside the vortex at the centre, spiralling in and out of existence, and pulling you towards the source of your creativity. You see before you a vision. Long pause here.

Were you carried along by the energy or could you control where the flow was moving? An ending and a beginning are signified here so give yourself a moment to say goodbye to whatever you are leaving behind, that no longer serves you. Pause here

As you look directly into the mirror of the universe what do you see?

After a significant pause here count down 4, 3, 2, 1 and come back to the room and waking consciousness.

10. *The Wheel of Fortune and Fate*

The Wheel of Fortune and Fate

This stage in the journey is where you can begin to instigate real and lasting change. On the image you can see a vortex and a spinning golden wheel. The symbols for the four fixed signs of the zodiac, Aquarius, Taurus, Scorpio and Leo are shown as the stars of those constellations. As I discussed earlier in the text you move through the zodiacal signs during the course of the inner spiritual journey. A personality can traverse through each of the signs, one at a time, and can transcend all of the characteristics held within each sign during these awakenings. You are able to experience all of the signs and not just the sign under which you were born. Within the Tarot it is this awakening process which concerns 12 Tarot archetypes that have their associations with 12 of the major arcana beginning with Aries and ending in Pisces.

There is a stage in the journey here during which you must visit each of the astrological signs on the inner plane. You must awaken each of these within your personality, and must integrate those experiences as they are reflected back at you in the physical world. This is the beginning of the process of spiritual alchemy.

Aries – God of the Grove / Emperor
Taurus – Shaman / Heirophant
Gemini – Lovers
Cancer – Chariot
Leo – Strength / Fortitude
Virgo – Hermit (son of the mother)
Libra – Lady Justice

Scorpio – Death

Saggitarius – Art of temperance

Capricorn – Pan / Hermes / Devil

Aquarius – Star Sothis

Pisces – Goddess of the Grove / Empress

This movement through the stages is a cyclical process and if you lay out the Major Arcana in the lemniscate or infinity pattern with the loop crossing at number ten. You will get an idea of the involutionary and evolutionary arc that makes up the whole journey. Further on in this book, at the Drowned or Hanged Man, the experience is one of the world being literally turned upside down, or going through a ritual initiation and wilful death to the personality, so as to be able to birth a new one. But in order to do this the tower must fall and the previous understanding of self and place in the world is shattered. Illusions are broken down.

Become the Hero/Heroine, set out on the quest or the journey to find your true self and it takes you through the Moon. In the Chariot of the Moon you must head into the underworld seeking the shadows. Once in the shadows the quest is for the inner sun or the sun at midnight, to be able to regain your self or whole personality.

The path of judgement comes when it is time to review one's life and make changes accordingly, after hearing the call to work with spirit. Stepping out into the world and treading on the fire path of spirit, the final stage. Then one whole cycle closes as the practitioner starts a new life after birthing from within, if they want they can return as the fool once more at the beginning of a new cycle.

There is so much more to the human experience that simply goes unnoticed by a large percentage of the population for whatever reason, and also a silent acceptance that the physical world is all that there is. These journeys and the experiences within the subtle realms, are in my opinion just as important as those of say going to university to study for a particular career. How can you understand how you affect other people's lives with your own actions if you do not even know yourself well enough to have journeyed within, met and talked with all of the different parts of yourself?

Everyone knows about karma, or the idea that how you treat people will directly reflect back at you in your life experiences, but how many people actually put this to work in their lives? Not for what we will get back in return but for purely creating a better world around us. To take the conscious choice in everything that we do and to consider what the consequences may be before acting, and not afterwards.

"Knowing" yourself is to take responsibility for all of your actions, the good ones as well as the bad. There is nothing to stop you doing something to put right any mistakes you may have made in the past instead of turning it into regret or psychic junk.

As above, so below, as within so without!

Making lasting changes to yourself is not an easy process and alchemy of your own personality takes time, effort, persistence, determination and willpower. If every person took a good hard look at themselves and honestly started to change themselves for the better, how do you think this would affect the way things are in the world? Making the choice to see things as they really are, becomes an important part of the focus at this point in the spiritual journey. Yes we are all different but we also share a lot of common things. Significant problems can arise if you begin to think you are better than, or at least not equal to each other. The idea of past lives is something I would like to cover briefly in this explanation of the "Wheel" which specifically deals with the idea of karma. Sometimes feeling of deja vu occur and the feeling that you have been here before. I'm sure it can be readily explained by science, but for the purpose of this text let's assume that consciousness is something that does not die and that it is a part of you and you are a part of it. Imagine your lives within lives that you have experienced so far and that the act of becoming, or waking up , as it has been termed in the alternative movement, is a crucial point in that journey. Where you understand that this life, the one you are living now, is the only one that you can ever make a difference to. Because the past has gone and the future hasn't happened yet and that you are living in the eternal now.

If you find yourself facing the same situations over and over again but with different players, you will then have to look at the patterns and analyse what you have not learned yet. You will then need to make changes accordingly so that you do not keep repeating the same mistakes again and again.

A Tibetan idea of the *"Wheel of Samsara"* presents the wheel as the journey of living, the experiences that happen to you while you are on the wheel of life, or in the physical world. You do not want to repeat over and over the same lessons and mistakes. You must consciously choose to direct your life towards cleaning up your lot and not making the same mistakes over and over. So that when you do finally come to leave this plane of existence you can do so with a clean slate, and an enlightened exit without any karmic baggage that is going to drag you back down here to go through it all again.

You could think of this as an extension of the choices presented earlier on in the journey during the lover's transition, when the road forked into a choice between a material and a spiritual existence. Only this time, the focus is upon the manifestation of your heart's desires or your worst nightmares, as a projection of your very soul essence into the world with the situations you are faced with in life. If you didn't learn the lesson the last time karma presented you with the opportunity to learn, while you are still here have another go. On some of the traditional imagery for this card we see the Sphynx and the image of the Hermanubis, or the one who tempts. The Sphynx represents traditions that have gone before us, lineages that we gravitate towards and the figures of Anubis and Typhon appear on some cards to signify good and evil.

Culture moves quickly and ideas rise and fall like the building of and the destroying of sacred temples. So the lesson which you need to learn here is one of morals and principles, right action and right choices from a place of wisdom. Deliberately choosing to leave the world behind you as a better place than it was before you awakened in it.

The Wheel or Chakra can be a understood as a representation of your life or the world in which you live, and everything that is in it has been drawn to you or repelled from you, by your conscious and unconscious thoughts, desires and actions. What ye sow, ye shall reap!

Questions

Are there cycles or patterns in your life that keep repeating? Where are you right now on the scale of happiness? Does your wellbeing hinge upon the thoughts or opinions that others hold about you? How much of what is in your life is there because you have consciously drawn it towards yourself and how much is there because of patterns repeating and destructive cycles that need to be broken?

Justice –
Invoking Sekhmet and restoring Maat

Take a deep breath and begin to relax. Start breathing in and out to the count of four. Once you are in your calm state of reverie we can begin. The darkness wraps itself around you like a blanket of the night sky. You are walking along a paved path which is illuminated although you cannot tell where the light is coming from. You don't see anything other than the path beneath your feet but you know where you are going. Follow your intuition to the sacred sanctuary at the end of the path. Pause here

You reach a building that is lit by torches either side of a raised doorway. Begin walking up some steps leading into a temple. It is still and peaceful inside, and the floor feels cold. In front of you there are two columns either side of another set of stone steps which you begin to climb. When you reach the top of the platform you are confronted with a great stone statue of a female figure holding a set of scales. She sits alone in this sanctuary raised on a dais. Torches adorn all of the inside walls of the temple and underneath your feet you see scattered reeds and marsh grass. Up above you the ceiling is painted in a precious midnight blue with stars and birds adorning every available space. There is a stone chair in front of this colossal figure and you turn your back to sit down. You converse with the energy that this great statue is projecting. Calm and serenity washes over you in a sensation like you are being cleansed by a cool shower. *Long pause here.*

Call upon Sekhmet to help you.

You hear a strong female voice speaking to you, 'you must restore balance'. Spend a few moments aligning with balance. If there is anything that you need to let go of. Do this now. *Pause*

Give silent thanks and remember everything you have experienced while you have been in this sacred space. Get up from the stone chair, bid farewell for now and walk back down all of the steps to the doorway. You hear a trickle of running water and look around for the source of the sound. As you stand in the doorway you notice that the whole of the building is now surrounded by a sacred lake. You can hear water trickling into the lake from lots of different places.

You smile as this reminds you of the river meeting the sea and you feel the calm serene peace once more. As you walk away from this temple you feel almost as if you have been given a new lease of life, and that the gates have opened, releasing an unstoppable force of energy that you only have to seek within. As you walk down the path, pause, look back, take one last glance and see the torches flickering, reflecting on the water that surrounds the temple. You feel renewed and come back with inspiration to put your affairs in order.

When you are ready open your eyes and record everything that you can remember of your experience within the temple.

11. Justice - Invoking SEKHMET and restoring MAAT

Justice - Change and transition phase

Here is an aspect of the goddess partially revealed. She is the goddess Sekhmet and it is her function to help you restore MAAT or balance. During this stage in the journey you begin to weigh your actions, against the motivations behind what you do and who you are. She pours clarity into the space around you and revelation into any difficult situations you may be facing. She also reveals plain truths to you whether you are ready to hear them or not. She is truth and fairness and this power unleashed, cuts through to the core. The Goddess Sekhmet is balancing the scales and she wields the sword of Truth, by the power of the intellect, bringing clarity, fairness and justice.

This is a transitional phase where you are neither within or without and you have the choice whether or not, to willingly submit yourself fully to the process of karmic cleansing which began in the last image of the Wheel of Fortune. The idea of the soul going into a hall of judgement is presented here, whereby your actions, deeds and intentions can be weighed against the heart. This is not necessarily the judgement that one might expect at death when you review the whole of your life, but a cyclical review, which relates directly to the time of year associated with this image, that of October and the beginning of autumn in the northern hemisphere. Let us briefly consider the concept of the Pagan new year at Samhain, as it is the "summers end" and time for the seasons to change.

Symbolic and seasonal death is upon us as the leaves fall from the trees and you begin the descent into the darkness of winter.

Your internal link with nature means that at this time of year, as the nights are closing in, subconsciously the waning sunshine hints to your waking self that the time is ripe for heading into retreat and repose. You should be allowing yourself the space to take stock of where you are, getting rid of the physical things you don't need anymore by giving them away to those who do. This is the time for ridding yourself of any beliefs that don't fit because you have grown. Setting out goals for the next year ahead and most importantly, taking the time out to remember your ancestors and the life that they gave you. In these times, sadly the commercialism of Halloween or Samhain has distracted many from its true meaning, in much the same way as the magic of the Winter Solstice has been lost inside the materialistic giant that is Christmas.

Your ancestral genealogy made you who you are today genetically, physically, emotionally, spiritually and otherwise; making you the bearer of those memories and lives which brought you into existence. Your family who have passed, now live in your memories and in your heart, yet they are still there at the central core of your being. You cannot run from who you are, and your family history is something that should be venerated and explored as much as possible. Teaching children about those figures who were once the head of generations past, who paved the way before you could begin to tread a path of your own destiny. Is something you could endeavour to participate in every year at the festival of celebrating the dead. Remembering where you come from, and getting to know your roots is a crucial stage in your personal and spiritual development.

How can you know who you truly are unless you have explored where and from whom you originated. Sometimes there may be karma that requires healing from past generations and it may manifest as difficulties in this life which appear to be out of your control. Talents and abilities that have skipped generations may lie dormant just waiting to be accessed, remembered and brought to life. Once you have been made aware of certain family traits that have run through the generations of those who laid the path for you. Make time to remember and honour your ancestors.

At the time of my writing this situations were only just swinging back into balance after being most assuredly out of kilter for quite some time. There was a period of learning painful lessons, letting go of the old to make way for the new and accepting that there are certain patterns that must be broken down in order make way for more healthy ways of living. The changing of lifestyles to those that are more suited to personal circumstances, psychological, emotional, and spiritual needs as well as physical needs. Most importantly leaving behind the residue of the past so that it no longer affects the present life, in the form of emotional baggage its attachments to people or negative situations that seek to thwart personal development and progression in life.

Call upon Sekhmet to clear out everything that is currently holding you back and be ready to accept full responsibility for all that you attract, they being conscious choices that bring you towards what you need in order to progress. The desired outcome is the restoration of peace, order and balance. Crowley called this card adjustment and hinted towards one of the suggested interpretations as a woman satisfied or fulfilled. We could take this one step further and say that here is the image of one who has discovered their personal power. She who understands the process of birth, life and death and as a result of this knowledge and wisdom has gained greater clarity. Taking full responsibility for all of your actions requires great courage and strength that can only be found within.

Questions

Are there situations in life that you could have handled better? What do you need to clear out in order to progress? Are you in balance or in chaos? What steps do you need to take now in order to regain composure and harmony with those around you?

Drowned Man

You are walking along a beaten coastal pathway through dry grasslands next to a calm sea. The tide is gently encroaching and the movement of the waves catches your attention. The deep blues and greens of the ocean waves ride in and out pulling shells and pebbles back and forth in its wake.

The colours around you are so vibrant and radiant that you feel as if you have just awakened inside a technicolour dream. It is a cold but bright and sunny autumnal day and there is a chill in the breeze which caresses your face. It feels as if you have been walking on the path for a long time. There is now a change in atmosphere and the passage of time and everything around you begins to slow down, almost like the Universe has gone on pause. Everything around you reaches a still point apart from the sensation of a pulse. You feel tired from your journey and look for a comfortable space to lie down.

The world around you is still and nothing moves anymore. With each breath that you take you become more aware of the rhythmic pulsations, fluctuations in the static, as the air around you takes on a different quality. You can sense the breath of the earth and are filled with the silence of a vast open space like a void around you. As you lie on the grass in this comfortable space something strange begins to occur. You feel as if the world is turning upside down and even though you can feel that you are lying on your back, it is as if you are nose to nose with the earth facing the ground.

You have changed your perception and begin to sink, passing through the earth, beginning a journey into the underworld. The sensation is like that of moving through a mirror and looking out at where you were from the other side. *Pause here*

You feel a deep connection with every living thing as your presence begins to attune to a different frequency and you resonate with the gentle motion of the waves lapping in and out at the waters edge. The wind has begun to pick up momentum and force as you are poised here in this suspended space, on the other side of your mirrored reflection in the underworld.

Far away in the distance you hear the sound of two ravens calling your name and a tempest begins to stir within you, as you gather your energies and move fully into the underworld. All that is unknown to you currently will be revealed as you begin your adventure. The ravens awaken within to bring you a greater understanding of the function of mind and memory. You are in control of the flow of information that you receive now and can allow your vision to come to you. *Long pause here.*

You ride the waves of the storm as the whirling winds lift you into a space where you can view your current path and journey through all that you have experienced up until this point in time. You have been taken to a different level of awareness and perception where you have much greater clarity and vision. Take a little time to get accustomed to this. *Pause here*

Bring back with you everything that you have experienced on your journey, back to the waking world. See yourself returning to the path beside the sea and then walking back to the place you started your journey. Become aware of your surroundings in the present moment. Clap your hands, stamp your feet. Make sure you are fully grounded in the present moment.

Write down any symbols, experiences, words, thoughts or pictures that may have emerged during your experience. The images that rise from our dream state while we are conscious can be of great importance to us, especially when we are in the process of finding our place and our calling in this life. Sadly at this stage in the journey many turn back because they are not ready to go within and face their own demons.

Drowned Man – Odin – Christed one

You are dealing here with a reversal of the ordinary and a completely different perspective from that which you are used to. The fact that the figure is hanging upside down and doesn't look at all bothered about it, suggests that this has been a voluntary course of action and a self sacrifice for the greater good. You could say that it is a willingness to immerse ones self in the true nature of things, in order to achieve and complete the great work that we are all capable of. This is the image of the Mystics and those who are unafraid to travel in the shadow lands, to further understand their place in the world and the nature of things.

In some decks the figure is poised with one leg crossed at the knee resting behind the other which forms the symbol for sulphur, suggesting the attainment of or reaching for the completion of something. The connecting of spirit within and without, the god-consciousness or however you decide to look at it in terms of your own understanding. You are suspended at this point in the spiritual journey as you question everything, including your reasons for being, and the surrendering of yourself to that which is bigger than you, and for the greater good of all. Knowing your place in the world however obscure that may seem to others around you and trusting that once you have answered that higher calling and begin to step out on your own and with the acceptance of responsibility for yourself, even though the journey may not be as easy as you thought it might be.

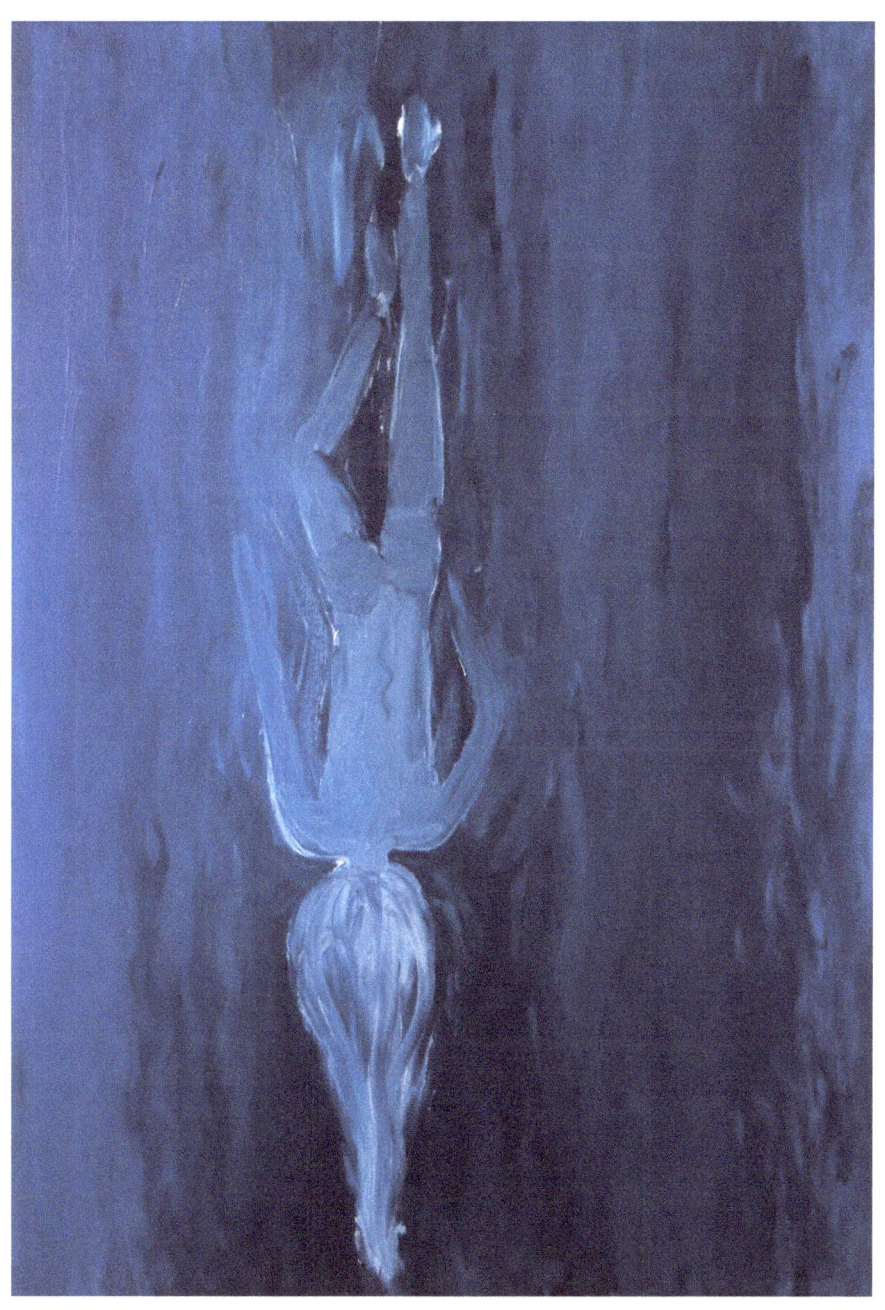

12, Drowned Man – Odin – Christed one

Some people at this stage in the spiritual journey walk away from their calling because they don't feel strong enough to endure the actions of others that come from a place of intolerance or ignorance. You have to trust that the awakenings or passive initiations which can result from this stage and onwards in the journey, are happening for a reason. Though you may not understand them at the time, as with anything, there will be experiences that will stay with you forever. You will find yourself changed beyond recognition because once you start to see things differently there is no turning back.

It is no coincidence then that in other decks there are names such as the hanged man or there are associations with Odin. As in myth, he willingly hung from the tree to receive the wisdom and knowledge of the runes, but at the price of sacrificing an eye. The intimation of a sacrifice is required here before one can progress any further. It is a voluntary submission and with the trusting that once you have passed through these experiences associated with the awakenings, you then come away from this with a greater understanding of the nature of Sacrifice. You can examine the endless possibilities available to you. What could you surrender or lose in order for you to receive more wisdom, understanding and clarity? Understand that fear is simply a component within the makeup of a human personality, that once established breeds more of itself if you allow it into your consciousness at any level. Fear of anything is a cage or a prison that you must break out of in order to have any chance at being truly alive.

How many people do you know that will not take action for *fear* that something bad might happen, or that someone will react badly as a result? This is no way to live and in choosing your own unique path you will require time away from the distractions of the modern world and to the those who are completely immersed in it, that choice will appear foolish and downright insane.

The very idea of the Tarot as the Path of the Fool or as a journey from innocence and ignorance to revelations, deeper meaning and to experience the mysteries of life, are summed up in this curious archetype. The inversion of the figure suggests that to attain the heights of wisdom, it is necessary to turn upside down worldly priorities, leaving behind the pursuit of wealth and status in order to attain the alchemical gold which can only be sought through the purification of the soul.

Eternal life is implied here in the sense that who we are and what we do will continue to live on long after we have shrugged off our mortal coil. In choosing to enter the shadow realms we are opening ourselves up to more experiences in life, because up until this point we may not have even been aware of these other worlds, beings, guides and the subtle realms that exist in their own right. While writing this part of the book I was exploring the Greek Myths a little which is not something I had done before. The one thing which struck me as interesting was the humanisation of the Gods. Why did the creators of these Myths bring the Gods so much closer to us by giving them human like forms? Do we create the gods or do they create us?

Are Gods and Goddesses something to be feared and revered? Or can we simply reverse this process and see them as inner sources to be contacted and consulted, while also revered and used as a tool to aspire towards their god and goddess-like natures!

In readings when this card appears. it can signify that the person is ready for deeper introspection and the turning away from material pursuits. Also, and most importantly, to pursue an inner journey or series of mystical experiences, as a result of getting more involved in spiritual matters. It can also mean entering into mystical states of awareness, with revelations, deeper insight into the inner worlds. And transformative and healing experiences that will bring much needed relief after periods of turmoil or stifled development.

Questions

Are you ready to know more about what lies in the deep recesses of your subconscious mind? To learn about the layers of content that are just below the surface of your conscious awareness? Are there patterns to your behaviour that could have been family traits? When you dream are there recurring images, places and people that you recognise but can't quite put a name to? Spend a little time journalling about these questions.

Death – Past Life Journey for Transformation

I want you to relax your body. Take in nice deep breaths and I want you to imagine that there is a bright sun shining down on you. You feel the warmth of the sun on your skin and I want you to let all the cares and worries of the day go, as you drift into this feeling of warmth. You see a clear blue sky above you and you feel the warmth of the sun and relaxation as this heat comes down to your head. You feel it spread down to your shoulders and travels though your chest in to your stomach. You feel healing warmth as it continues to travel down your spine, softening all the muscles as you relax.

This warmth spreads and flows through your hips, thighs and legs down into your ankles. It is such a relaxing and comforting warmth. Every breath you take is a signal to go deeper and deeper relaxed into this state of peace. Just listen to the instructions and the sound of my voice. Allow yourself to be led to a calm meditative state. Give yourself permission to totally relax. With every breath you get more and more relaxed.

Ask now for your shield or your guardian angel, your ancestors and spirit guides to come forward and journey with you to help you, to remember anything you see or hear. Ask them to clarify anything that you don't understand. All you need to do is relax.

Take yourself to your sacred space. All your senses are keen and aware in this space. Allow each breath to take you deeper and deeper. As you become more and more relaxed with each breath, you go deeper and deeper relaxed.

With every breath you sink even deeper into total relaxation.

Now that you are in your sacred space you look around and notice a path that you haven't seen before. You are surrounded by a beautiful woodland near a winding river. Have a good look all around at the trees and the colours. As you follow this path alongside the river feel your connection with mother nature strengthen. You notice your heightened sensations. Somewhere in the distance you become aware of the sound of water growing louder. As you follow the river to the source, you find a waterfall and healing pool. Walk now alongside the beautiful pool, and you become aware of a rainbow shining above. Feel the soothing energy as you step into the healing waters. Pause a moment here

When you are ready step out of these healing waters and walk towards another path, this will lead you into an ancient forest. The lush greenery is all around you. Feel the warmth and the inviting atmosphere as you venture further into this ancient woodland. Ahead of you there is a clearing and a structure in the clearing. This building is your very own, private, sacred, temple. Continue to make your way towards the building and remember what it looks like. As you get closer you become aware of a profound sense of peace and unity. Spend a moment taking in all the details of the shape, size, entrances and remember what it looks like. Pause here.

Remember where the doors and windows are. Take a moment to walk around the outside, taking in all the details, then return to the front of the building where the entrance is and place your hand on the door. How does it feel? Remember every detail. This building is very special. It contains records of all of your past lives.

It holds everything you have ever learned or experienced right up to the present moment. When I count to three you are going to push open the door and go inside. Ready? 1,2,3. Notice the change you experienced as you walked through the door. Become aware of the surroundings inside. What do you see? Remember everything. I'll give you a moment to do this now. Long pause.

You are slowly engulfed by a fine violet mist. It wraps itself around you, and when the mist begins to clear it reveals a beautiful staircase with ten steps leading down into a hallway. I'm going to count you down the steps now. 10,9,8,7,6,5,4,3,2,1

You are now standing in the long hallway. There are lots of doors to your left and your right. Some of them are lit up from behind. Feel yourself being drawn towards a particular door. Ask for your guides and ancestors to draw in close and accompany you on your journey. Become aware of their presence. Behind this door is one of your past lives. You can move forwards and backwards through this life with just a thought. If your body feels uncomfortable at any point you can draw down the warm healing energy from your head and breathe through any discomfort.

I'm going to count to three now and you will step through the door.
Ready
1,2,3

Remember any thoughts and feelings and energies that arise. What do you need to know about this life? Allow your emotions to come to you as you have this experience. Pause here.

Now I want you to focus on your feet. What are you standing on? Are you wearing anything on your feet. Can you tell the colour of your skin? Are you wearing any clothes? Can you perceive a gender? Take a moment to find out who you are. Any details. Remember everything. Place your hands out in front of you and look at the detail. Scan your body for information and slowly become aware of your surroundings. Are you inside or are you outside? What does the temperature feel like? Allow yourself to go deeper and deeper into the experience and immerse yourself in it. Pause here.

Move now to the evening of the same day. You are sitting down for a meal. Are you alone? What are you eating? You become aware of the life circumstances. You hear your name being spoken. Remember everything and bring it back with you. Become aware now of anyone that you recognise as being part of your life. What relationship do you have with this person? Focus on their face.

You can move now to the entrance to the house where you live in this life. Remember every detail and remember how you feel. How does your body feel? See yourself enter and go from room to room. Do you have a favourite place? Notice every detail. Is there a particular object you would like to bring back with you. Pause here.

Come away from that experience and move on to any unresolved conflict you might have had. Ask your guides and ancestors to come in close and allow those images to arise. You can now perceive any significant events that are related to this experience. These also might be replaying in your life now. All the while remember that you are safe, secure, relaxed and at peace. Bring all the images back with you to your present life. You can do this now. Pause here.

Ask your guides to show you the connections between the situations you are seeing and what is now happening in your current incarnation. Ask for clarity and guidance so you can understand why these things are happening. Pause here.

I want you to move to the day when you died in this lifetime. No pain, no fear, just experience that time in which you died. Become aware of how old you are. Are there people with you? Scan your mind back and realise the cause of your death and anything that you brought with you from that lifetime into your present life. Allow yourself to let go of any regrets or issues. You can let go of them all now. Imagine yourself moving through the death experience and leaving the body. See yourself free, unrestricted, and able to move on.

Use your intuition and ask your guides to take you on this final stage of the journey. It's time for you to ask "What do you need to know from this life? And what do you need to teach others?"

Become aware of any decisions that you made in that life time that are affecting you now. What advice can you give yourself to help you with your present incarnation? Recognise now what you are here to achieve in your current incarnation, what your life purpose is.

Relax and remember these things. Pause here

Over the next few days and weeks you will receive more information about your past lives and memories will surface, bringing information and healing. When you go to sleep tonight become aware of accessing past life information in your dreams. You will remember easily and you will be able to record the information when you wake up. Quickly scan your body for any areas of tension and allow them to dissolve. You have no need for blocks any more. It is time for you to go back to your sacred building. Back to your healing space bringing with you all the information you have experienced. Know that over the next few days you will keep remembering. Become aware of your body and the floor underneath you. You now here in your present incarnation. Awake.

(Adapted from a Past Life Workshop given by Deborah Monshin)

Death - Past Life Journey for Transformation

Anyone who has experienced a death in the family will tell you of the affect it has on perception. For a brief moment there is an appreciation of the life that you have, perhaps even a radical change occurs in which the death brings mental clarity upon what is important in life.

The death image in the Tarot can be thought of as an analogy of what the actual sun in the sky is to life on Earth, the constant power source that waxes and wanes throughout the agricultural year. In turn it has a subtle effect on physical bodies as well as moods, emotions and thoughts which may be dependent on what stage of the year the sun is passing through.

You constantly change as a human being and you do not have the same identities all throughout your life. The death of the ego can lead you into the process called the "Dark Night of the Soul" and this is something which is not to be taken lightly. When you go through this process you experience a cleansing from within and literally you become someone else, because the personality that existed before that ego death has been purged. This can be uncomfortable for friends and loved ones as they watch this person they think that they know, changing like a chameleon before their eyes into a different person. Change is one of the only constants in life and once this is accepted, nothing is ever going to stay the same and you can willingly move into a different perspective. One that accepts and embraces change and the rise and fall of tides and cycles that you will experience during these times.

You have been born into one life when you come to this plane of manifestation and at this point in the spiritual journey you can choose to re-create yourself magically. You can rebirth your personality as you begin to integrate your higher self more and more into your waking life, then after rebirthing yourself by going through an initiation or ordeal in which you allow oneself to die and completely recreate yourself anew.

This is one of the most misunderstood cards in the deck by those who don't know a great deal about the Tarot. There is often an assumption and irrational fear that it means that the person who draws this card is going to die. This is because a lot of people are afraid of dying, let me re-assure you that it is very rare that drawing this card during a reading means that you will literally be leaving this physical plane altogether. Sometimes it can represent the pain of separation from someone close when they have moved on but more frequently it denotes drastic change in one form or another. Loss of a long term relationship perhaps. The death that is required is an ego death and its subsequent built up persona. There is no need to wear a mask of projection and the self murder that is rife in our society can be realised, if you choose not to ignore the stirrings of your true nature. Once you have passed through this part of the spiritual journey, you can bring to life the seed of the real person which has lain dormant inside for so long. Ignited you can birth this new part of yourself and become who you were truly meant to be. There is nowhere to hide from the real you and once you realise and accept this then you can begin the process of refinement of your personality.

Burning away the dross of ideas and perceptions that have built up like stagnant layers over the years. Once alight this spreads like wildfire to cleanse the personality of its accumulated bad

13. Death – Past Life Journey for Transformation

habits, negative associations, self deception and abuse of ones own character. Dramatic change is required here. So in light of the text earlier on about the High Priestess and the three faces of the goddess, this card is very much centred in the crone aspect of the triple goddess who stands at the doorway of Death. In nature the seasons are in a perpetual motion of change and if you align yourself with the natural world, then in November as the leaves are falling from the trees and the scent of Winter is upon you, your thoughts and ritual naturally turn towards remembering the dead. The loved ones who have passed. Internally you can begin to let go of the parts of yourself that no longer define who you are. In the increasing darkness you are forced to look into the shadows and confront your fears, boldly journeying within and seeking out those dark places where you keep your memories, good or bad, and you must process some of the things that lay buried in the deepest recesses of the mind. Hidden content that could be hindering your spiritual progression, even though you may not be consciously aware of them. There is so much more to you as a human being than simply your thoughts, feelings and connections with other people.

Consider past lives for a moment. Stories that are consistently reported where children have memories of places and people from a life that they claim to have consciously lived before the present one.

Even down to being able to supply details of places and people that can be referenced and have been found to be real people, that were not just a figment of the child's imagination. Much has been written about the possibility of emotional 'disorders' and the onset of a disease having their beginnings in unresolved conflict at the time of death in a past life. Not everyone is able to access past life information, let alone even entertain the notion. For the purpose of this part of the spiritual journey it may be prudent to do a little bit of research and meditation on your pre-birth plans. Especially if you are not aware of your higher calling or purpose in life. It could be that you need to do some inner work to clear unresolved issues, before you can access the hall of records. To bring through information into your conscious awareness of previous lives, to gain more insight on what you are supposed to be doing in this life.

Even if you don't believe that this is possible you could still use the past life meditation exercise metaphorically, to work through any of the issues that have been highlighted during the meditation process.

The appearance of this card in a reading suggests the need to embrace the shadow self and accept that there has to be darkness with the light. To work towards acceptance of parts of the self that require nurturing and begin the process of alchemy to change from within.

Questions

Who are you really? How well do you know your ancestry and family lineage? Do you have roots in a particular spiritual tradition or are you actively seeking a tradition? Are you ready to let go of the past and turn your attention to the present moment and what you can do now?

Temperance

It is time now to go to a place deep within and contemplate your journey so far. You are walking through a deserted wasteland and it feels empty and desolate. You are searching and seeking something yet you are unaware of what lies ahead of you. As you walk, your thoughts turn towards all the different experiences that you have had so far along this journey. As images begin to flicker in your mind's eye of all the places that you have visited here, you stop walking because there is something different happening on the landscape right in front of you now.

Before your eyes you see a silvery outline of a tunnel which forms out of thin air. It begins to take on substance and before you know it you are standing in front of a huge cave-mouth opening. You look behind you at the waste land that has brought you to this point while wandering, and then turn again to look at the inviting cave in front of you. Take a few steps into the darkness.

It is still, silent and peaceful. The darkness has a quality to it that is alive. The further you walk, the brighter the inside of the cave becomes even though you cannot perceive a light source. The walls are glistening and you sense a presence that reaches out to you which feels familiar, magical and comforting, beckoning you to venture further into the darkness. Beings of all the colours of the rainbow make themselves known to you and you can safely immerse yourself in their protective light.

As your eyes become accustomed to the strange light you see that there is a large stone chair in the middle of the cave, which looks like it has been carved out of age old stalacmites and fossils. You make your way to the chair and sit down. A shiver passes through you and you sit quietly in contemplation within this sacred place. Pause here.

After a while you begin to notice that there are carvings and symbols on the walls of the cave and you feel like you need to investigate further. Pause Here

Even though you are alone in this semi-darkness you can sense that you are surrounded by the presence of the masters and ancestors who have gone before you and you realise that their knowledge is etched into the very fabric of this place. If you listen very carefully you will hear them as they all speak to you with one voice. Take some time to be still and to receive the guidance and healing that you need right now. Long Pause

When you are ready and it is time to emerge from your introspection, you walk back to the cave entrance and stand for a moment looking out at the landscape. You see that it has changed from one of emptiness and desolation to a thriving symphony of sound. It is dusk and all the night creatures have begun to stir and awaken. Insects chatter and somewhere in the distance you hear an owl hooting a greeting to you, as she glides through the trees on her way out to hunt. Know that you are never walking this journey alone and on these many paths you travel, your guides are always here to show you the way.

Feel yourself coming back to waking consciousness with all of the guidance and wisdom that you have received.

Don't forget to record any signs, messages, or insights you had during the meditation in your journal along with any inspirations you may have received.

The Art of Temperance

The "Art of Temperance" heralds the beginning of a process which requires bravery on the part of the seeker for it means putting yourself into the cauldron of regeneration. This may take years or months once the process has begun, as each and every person going through the experience will have different life circumstances and progression. So what occurs slowly for one person over a lifetime may happen in a short space of time for someone else.

On early Tarot decks this image has an angelic figure pouring water between two vessels and is associated with the figure of Aquarius, the water bearer, with a foot on the land and a foot in the water. Endlessly transferring the living water between the two urns signifying the ebb and flow of life force in the individual concerned. On the Initiate's way image the angelic figure is facilitating the rebirth of the individual in the cauldron, by breathing out the phoenix at the end of the process of alchemical transformation.

Consciously put yourself into this cauldron and choose what it is that you want to change. You can begin by asking the cauldron for a gift. If the gift that you wish for is success then you will have to be prepared to put in the work and the effort, as that will also be required for you to bring it to fruition. It's no good asking for fame and fortune then sitting back and waiting for the process to happen all of its own accord!

The cauldron is the source of inspiration, creativity, wisdom and knowledge and before you can put yourself in it you have to know where to find it! The cauldron is the vas; the womb of the great Mother, and through her you can recreate your world through

14. The Art of Temperance

the art of temperance. Change and realisation of the great work rises from the cauldron and rainbow light streams out to form the androgynous figure of the radiant being which can be found on my previous image of the Art in the Soulscapes Tarot.

You are required at this stage to spend time journeying into the core of the Earth and seeking out the guides and ancestors who guard the caverns below. At the time of painting this magical image I was regularly performing the 'mount of illumination' meditation by Dion Fortune. On one occasion I went up to the library during the meditation and took a book off the shelf to read entitled "Alchemie" and spent a good while there absorbing information from the book about the process of Alchemy. The latin phrase which is inscribed on the cauldron was repeated to me for the duration of the meditation like a chant!

> VISITA INTERIORA TERRAE RECTIFICANDO INVENIES OCCULTUM LAPIDIEM
> V.I.T.R.I.O.L
> 'Visit the interior parts of the Earth; by rectification thou shall find the hidden stone'
> – Aleister Crowley *The Book of Thoth*.

There is a connection with Sagittarius and the arrow in flight, which can be understood as clear communication with the mercurial aspect of our minds. This allows us to create and sustain willpower over long periods of time, so that you can bring your creations from ideas to manifestation. Dion Fortune suggests that the mind of an initiate is likened to a diamond, and the process of shaping it until it is perfected, it then becomes a tool for the practitioner to use for the rest of their days to perform their 'great work'.

You must think of the fire element as purging and metaphorically cleansing the soul of all that is negative and unhealthy after introspection taking place, preferably during the longest night of the year at the winter solstice. The greatest obstacles to overcome are simply fear and anxiety, and never looking into the darkness in the first place because you are afraid of what you might find.

Fully immersing yourself into this experience will result in the incarnation or finding the light/star/diamond within your self. During the month of December 2016 I had an encounter on a deserted beach during which I was introduced to "Sothis" under a star studded moonless night. After a solitary ritual I was looking up to the stars in contemplation and heard that phrase whispered in my ear. When I returned home and did a little research on who or what was "Sothis" I was pleasantly surprised to find that it was another name for the star Sirius. There are also some interesting references to it as an astral being or god/goddess; an androgynous being that pervades the ether, like a guardian almost, or a sentry to the experiences that were to come over the next few months.

The Art of Temperance is a phase in life where you actively seek to attain walking a path of perfect balance within and without. So that you can step on to the rainbow path, and as you walk in harmony with the world around you life in the physical realm becomes a mirror of that balance point, and you can truly experience the glory of being. Limitations stem only from a lack of imagination of what you could achieve, or from thinking you don't have enough, and this could hold you back for years. Be free with your thinking. Think big and without limits.

Working with spirit in all of its forms brings a rich tapestry of experiences and limitless boundaries. You will begin to realise that the only thing that separates you from anything else is your attitude towards it. Be open to receive and embrace the unknown.

Here you stand on a plateau amongst the gods and goddesses with the stars shining down on you and the earth beneath your feet supporting you. You have a clear perspective that enables you to begin to make informed decisions about your own future with confidence and courage, and for the greater good and benefit of all. You feel the tide of the life force as it ebbs and flows and you begin to percieve the subtle changes in the ether before things happen. With your higher self to guide you, and your feet firmly planted on the ground, you can put your best foot forward and walk your dreams into reality one baby step at a time.

Questions

In the grander scheme of things are you ready to begin again from a completely different perspective and instigate change? Are you able to have direct conversation and guidance with your higher self? What do you need to do in your life so that you can put yourself in the right place spiritually, to get the best out of your time and draw towards you those who will enable you to fulfil your destiny?

Pan – Hermes - Devil (Guardian of the Earth)

(Light some dark green candles before performing this pathworking)

In the stillness, darkness and silence of the night you are wandering once again under a star studded sky. The moon is dark and the glory of the stars fills your senses. There is an icy chill in the air as you return to the Cave entrance that we visited in the last visualisation, but this time it feels slightly different. Once you see it fully formed step into the mouth opening. There is an altogether eerie presence as you enter the cave.

As there is no light, you are forced to use your bodily senses to move into the darkness and the shadows seem to encroach and move towards you as you walk into this vast dark space. You venture further into the inky blackness and you can just make out something glowing at the end of a small tunnel. You are drawn towards this faint orange glow issuing from a tiny seam of light which is seeping through the cracks of a heavy old wooden door. There is an ornate knocker on the door and you feel slightly unnerved because you don't know what is behind this door. The silence amplifies and you know that something is behind the door, because you feel it. Gather all of your courage and knock loudly. Pause

After a moment you hear a loud click as the door slowly creaks open. As you move into the chamber and the door closes behind you. In front of you there is a form chained to concrete blocks on the floor and a lit torch high up on the wall that illuminates the scene.

As you inch closer the fear begins to well up inside of you. What if this is a beast or a monster? The outline of the form becomes clearer now. You can now see two robed figures curled up together, on the floor with cobwebs and dust on the cloth of the robes and on the floor around them. As they become aware of your presence they lift up their heads to look at you. They look at you with interest as it has been a longtime since they had any company. A kindly green face materialises in your minds eye and he tells you that he is the guardian of this sacred place. He asks you what is it that you seek?

He tells you that you must become aware of the limitations, beliefs and temptations that are leading you astray. He asks you if you know yourself, who you really are and if you are ready to let go of the things that no longer serve you? He tells you that the figures chained before you are the *reflections of your self imposed constrictions and the attitudes that you have bound to yourself though they can be removed. As you listen to what he has to say the chains that you saw binding the forms to the floor begin to dissolve and you can feel your own burdens beginning to lift. He tells you that his job is to guide you back to the path where you went astray. All manifestation of things on Earth pass through this place. The beasts of the field, the birds of the air, and the fish of the waters are all companions on the Earth. He tells us it is our job to protect their home as it is also our home and we must share our existence with them, never dominating over them. He tells you that when you go through this door you will be ready to move on to the next part of your journey which involves breaking down the illusions held by the mind.*

The two forms in robes begin to rise and shed their garments to the floor. You watch as the two forms merge into each other and transform into the image of a radiant goddess. Your heart is filled with wonder and excitement. She has a message for you.

(Pause here.)

Now I want you to return with this blessing and the guidance received. When you are ready push open the large heavy door and walk back into the cave where you started your journey.

Take a few moments to process all of the information that you have been presented with and when you are ready come back to the room.

15. Pan – Hermes - Devil

Pan – Hermes – Devil

The central figurehead presented here is that of a guardian flanked either side by two faces of the goddess. In some versions of this card there is an image of a beastly form either cloven hoofed or with claws, often with a reversed pentagram somewhere within the picture. The idea being shown here is that of overcoming self limiting beliefs and personality traits that are less than desirable. Also changes in attitude from selfishness to altruism, and emphasising the need to consider nature as another species to form relationships with rather than to 'lord' over, or to perceive as being there purely as a commodity for humans.

Consider for a moment the mythology of the Horned God or Cernunnos and the Celtic idea of Cerridwen, or the Cauldron of inspiration which we were introduced to in the last image. The Horned God as the very essence of nature and the Cauldron containing the brew from which we return to again and again as the source for our ideas and imagination. Pan or the Devil is the manifestation of those ideas onto the physical plane via the creation of form. The alchemical process of 'Solve et Coagula' is the act of separation and analysis of all of the components or ingredients you have been stirring in the pot to bring something new into manifestation. In the last part of your journey you travelled within the 'hidden earth' to find the substances with which to re-create yourself anew. Now look carefully at all of those different pieces with scrutiny and put to the flame the parts that no longer serve, and you can now create the philosopher's stone; out of the darkness springs the eternal youth as a state of mind.

Pan as Lord of Arcadia is the guardian of hidden sanctuaries, caves, grottoes and places of worship that are, have been, and continue to be sacred to those who visit them as part of their cultural heritage. Unfortunately, over the years much misfortune has come to these physical places, especially during times when belief structures changed. In some traditions there is a belief that for Christ to be born, Pan had to die and perhaps this might explain the similarity of the dark renditions of the Devil as a monstrous creature and the later associations of this deity with Shaitan or Satan. The Roman equivalent of this horned one is that of a cloven hoofed faun who is one of the incarnations of Hermes wielding his magical staff.

Upon wild mountaintops, and lonely places, in sacred caves and grottoes you will find Pan, and in certain music which can cause changes in consciousness or at the very least arouse feelings of sexuality, desire or passion. Let us briefly consider the nature of sexuality for enjoyment and pleasure, metaphorical fertility to create yes but not purely for procreation and also the enjoyment of sexual pleasure without sin!

If we understand that the perfect union and balance between the male and female, as two parts of a whole being that come together to create a third state, that of ecstasy, this third state of being is one of polarisation. We have then a can of worms waiting to be opened when asking the question 'what happens to a physical body during years of suppression of this natural sexual instinct?'

Numerologically speaking we have a 1 and a 6 here, 1 is the number of the Magician and 6 is the number of the Lovers. Adding 1 and 6 together we get the number of the Chariot of the Moon, or number 7.

One of the subjects already touched on slightly in previous chapters is that of the creation of the Merkaba, which is the function and focus of the imagery portrayed in the chariot. Simply put the vehicle of the orgasm can be used as a tool for achieving altered and heightened state of awareness, which can be used for the creation of magical charges.

This archetype of Pan is connected with January and Saturn as the part of the year when in the gregorian calendar, the previous year is ending and another is beginning. The astrological sign associated with this image is that of Capricorn, or the mountain goat. The qualities you find when considering this image are that of stability, inner resources, down to earth with no nonsense attitudes and knowing yourself well enough to recognise what you are required to change in order to progress. Better the Devil you know.

You may also become painfully aware at this stage of time and all of its constraints. Time on earth is short and this is as good a time as any to reflect and consider are you doing all that you should be doing or have you gotten distracted along the way? Impulses and desires play a big part in the realisation process and taking responsibility for your choices and actions. Choosing whether or not to act on your impulses and what the outcome will be, considering possible outcomes beforehand and making sure that you are not setting yourself upon a road which could potentially be disastrous. Prioritisation is required between the needs and the wants, and what in reality can or cannot be achieved at present. Business and commerce are things to be considered at this stage also. The need to make money can be perceived as something which binds us, that is if we allow ourselves to become a slave to it.

On the other hand it can be that connecting with this image allows you to more fully understand the concept of attracting and handling of money in big business, and therefore making life more comfortable as a result of the work and effort that you put in. Any successful business person will tell you that time managed wisely and knowing when and where not to act are two of the main ingredients required for successful project management, that and human resources. Hermes as the god of commerce is a very apt association as being able to adapt to ones environment like the chameleon is priceless in terms of commerce, and knowing how to act in every situation from a place of calm and down to earth stability with an ability to foresee certain future events. Allows for planning projects ahead in accordance with the needs of those who would use the service or business.

Reorienting or reconsidering the importance of matters that involve land and land management, conservation of wildlife and projects that involve the restoration of land after having been reclaimed are matters that may come to the forefront at this time. Connecting with the goddess of the land or sacred spaces that have been left un-attended, or forgotten.

The appreciation of green spaces, planting new forests and woodlands, caring for wildlife sanctuaries or even establishing new sacred spaces where human and animal can meet as equals.

Questions

Are there places where you could make some time to seek out the grottoes of Pan, or local places where the Spirit of Nature can be sought for communion with this ancient deity? How in tune are you with your own sexuality, desires and the need to fulfil those, to maintain a healthy state of body and mind communication?

The Tower

You find yourself wandering along a deserted hillside and the sky above you is grey. Seagulls cry high up in the sky, circling and playing in the currents of the air high above. There is a storm brewing in the distance and we can feel the electricity building in the atmosphere as we journey along our path. As you walk you think about how far you have come and the changes that you have made so far. Think of all of the the masks that you have made and that you consciously project out in to the world so that people will see you a certain way, hiding parts of who you are for fear of rejection. As you walk and ponder you come to a cross roads in the path. The green track along which you were walking is interrupted by black pavement which cuts right through it.

Beside you there are stones and rubble which are the ruins of a fallen tower and you become aware of two guardians who have been waiting here to greet you. You are ushered to a stone chair amongst the debris and the guardians beckon you to sit down. The guardians tell you to imagine that you are inside of the tower as it once was and then it will be so. Create in your imagination now the image of a tall stone spiral tower in all of its former beauty. Pause a moment.

Now move inside the vision of the tower and begin to walk up the rough cut steps of the spiral staircase that lead up past sporadic torches which illuminate the way. As you climb higher you stop to look out of one of the windows and see that there is a mound in the distance glowing by the radiance of the stars.

Thunder rumbles in the distance and the wind has whipped into a fury outside as it whistles through the open windows. Momentarily you experience fear but the realisation comes to you that you are here for a reason, to reveal your true nature and break out of your self imposed prison. Lightening strikes illuminate the inside of the spiral tower and show you everything you have hidden from yourself. This is where your fears live. They build themselves up a brick at a time until you are afraid to act because of what might be. Another flash of lightening hits the tower and this time it *releases a great tension and all the blocks that you have created for yourself come tumbling down along with the rocks that have been dislodged with the storm. You are safely escorted back to where you began your journey among the ruins of the Tower, now confident in the knowledge that you have overcome fear and with clarity of perception are ready to go on with your exploration of the shadows.*

Don't forget to write down any thoughts or experiences immediately afterwards that you had during your journey.

The Tower of Illusion comes crashing down

The lightening of the tower often comes like a bolt from the blue to wake you from the sleepwalking state. Conflict and inner turmoil that require attention will arise now; clarity, perception and awareness come flooding in. There is no month attached to this image as it is a state of being that is changeable depending on where you are in your cycle of progress. Tension between opposing ideas or characteristics will present themselves during this awakening. Difficult decisions and often warring natures within your psychological makeup become increasingly evident as you plunge headlong into the experience of a fall from within the tower.

Self deception is one of the most common personality traits or defence mechanisms that can be rectified at this point in the spiritual journey. How many of your reactions to the world around you are based upon actual events, and do you have a clear perception of where you are, what you are doing and where you are going? Do you find that you act from past conditioning or because of negative experiences that have coloured the way you think about certain situations, people or events? You need to question why things make you feel the way you do. Are you getting all the facts or have you deluded yourself into thinking that things are a certain way just so that you don't have to deal with the cold hard reality. That you are just as much to blame for the situations that you find yourself in because what is happening around you and in your life is a reflection of your inner world!

16. The Tower

So if your life is chaotic and messy, your inner life needs attention to restore order to the chaos. Then in turn you can bring about changes in the world around you as you consciously change from within. Choosing to ignore warning signs or refusing to accept responsibility for one's own actions will inevitably lead to a breakdown of some sort. What is required of you here is to look at ways to instigate change regularly so that your life does not become stagnant and stuck. Building yourself up into a high tower creates the state of *Separatio* or sacred change, you have all of the separate pieces that are required and this phase, that is only temporary, is necessary. So that now you can release and let go of any previous misconceptions, out-moded ways of thinking and acting and make room for any changes that have been necessary for progression. Perhaps you have allowed fear to breed instead of having the courage to do what is required, to stand up with faith and conviction and to be true to who you should be, not a projection of that which has been created for the benefit of everyone else.

When you experience the death of a loved one it can pull you into a curious state where you are temporarily cut off from the living, as you say your goodbyes to the dear departed in a different place entirely. This has already been discussed but I mention it here because that state of being is akin to this process in your spiritual development journey at the falling tower. You have reached a point of no return in some aspect which has brought about dramatic change and for the better in the long run, but you may have been avoiding dealing with something up until this point.

When you begin to see the cracks appearing in life situations and notice the behaviour patters of yourself and other people around you, things that you may have been looking at with rose tinted spectacles up until this moment, suddenly become glaringly obvious. You may temporarily be 'shocked' by revelations that you just didn't see up until this point. In my own journey at this stage it was hard to see that I had been happily living a lie and that the foundation upon which I had been standing was never going to last. It was built upon false promises and was a self created prison under the guise of security. I was being given warning signs in my dreams but didn't pay attention to them until it was too late, and then the world I had known came tumbling down around me, forcing me to see the situation as it really was.

Events that cause a sudden shock and re-evaluation of life come under this arcana. So how do you survive this catastrophic event? You have to mould, shape and transform yourself into something else, for unless deception is uncovered and the untruths which have been hidden from you come to light, there can be no forward momentum. You cannot build stable foundations on unsteady ground, because it will eventually come crashing down. You need to learn to recognise shifting tides and live in harmony not only with those around you, but also with the universe itself and the earth upon which you tread.

Self discovery inevitably comes with shocking revelations and makes you look at cold hard facts, especially if you have been kidding yourself into acting out something that you are not, then the persona will crack and reality will intervene.

Until you make the effort to take responsibility for your part in the chaos and disruption and begin to work towards a much healthier viewpoint and perspective then this process will repeat indefinitely. Putting expectations on yourself or others and then finding out the hard way that the reality isn't living up to the image that is being projected from your mind. You set yourself up again and again to fall from the top of the tower that you have built around yourself. Sometimes it is built in defence after hard knocks in the past, so that you can hide away from situations that you are struggling to come to terms with. When you temporarily need to detach yourself, in order to gain a better perspective on how to fix a problem or see a better solution, rather than being caught up in the tide of drama. Remain centred, balanced and focussed through difficulties instead of reacting negatively to situations.

Whatever life throws at you, just remember you need these experiences and its lessons so that you can learn in terms of personal growth, and this process is priceless. Knowing whether or not to act and if you sense that something is coming then expect the unexpected and try to make the best out of these trying situations. Cultivate self love and protect yourself from harm and then ride out the storm.

There is great potential here for you to unleash power of your own and use it to move forward out of any danger, real, imagined or otherwise.

> "How do we survive, and thrive in the middle of this? By connecting with the cards alternative name, La Maison Dieu, the House of God. By living in harmony with the Universe, determining the mood of the times and going with it, by understanding who you are and what you are for, and by appreciating Cosmic Forces and withdrawing our investment from man-made forces then, even if the Tower falls, we may walk away unscathed. Cosmic forces come to disrupt the plans of men. In the life of nations expect the unexpected, back

the outsider, believe the impossible and trust nothing to chance." – Richard Abbot

Questions

Once you have the truth and you are aware of things that which were previously hidden from you, can you rebuild your thought space so that you don't become blinded again in the future? Is the fall a good or a bad thing in terms of lessons learned and progression that can be made afterwards? Next time you are faced with something that seems unsurmountable will you be able to stop and think, "What is actually going on here?", and allow the scales to fall away from your eyes and perceive reality?

The Star (Sothis)

Imagine that you are walking on frozen sand along a cold deserted beach underneath a canopy of glittering stars. It is February in the western hemisphere and the midnight blue and indigo of the horizon draws you into its beauty. The stars twinkle and gleam above you and the more you look at them the more of them you begin to see, almost as if they are popping into existence the more attention that you pay to them. One particular star catches your attention and you focus all of your energy and awareness on this bright glowing orb. You feel yourself moving towards it and you mentally call it closer and closer to you until you feel its presence begin to merge with your being.

You feel a tickling sensation on your forehead between your eyes as you immerse yourself in the beauty and radiance of the star. You become aware of a great being whose essence is the radiant night and you feel a protective cloak, woven from the sky being cast all around you. Silvery light radiates from within the being and you feel yourself merge with it. You become a radiant light emitting your pulse into the darkness. Anticipation grows, as does excitement and hope for the future that you are going to create yourself. This great star being being has a message for you and you take a moment to listen to what she/he has to say.

(Pause here.)

Bring back all of the information you have received with thanks and gratitude and record it in your journal.

17. *The Star Sothis*

The Star Sothis

During my own personal journey the presence of Venus was a constant companion in the sky when I was doing my pathworkings with the star Sothis. I would look out of the window and she always seemed to be there just as I was settling down to my inner work. The constellation of Orion also was a notable presence setting on the horizon in the South as I was painting and working on the star.

Where does inspiration come from? What motivates you to do the things that you do whether that is to create or to set out on new and untried paths? The stillness, serenity and peace of winter still holds a firm grasp during the arrival of snowdrops in the northern hemisphere. These are the days when the atmosphere is so still and there is no movement at all except the silent fall of snowflakes from the clouds. There is something truly magical in these peaceful moments and in the celebrations of Imbolc when lighting many lamps and candles and feeling the internal stirring of coming springtime.

After the destruction of the tower all you saw around you was debris and ruins and you were left in a very different place to that where you entered the experience. The mist has cleared from your eyes and you know now that there cannot be any deception of self. Acceptance and nurturing of that light that is inside of you that makes you unique, that is the very essence of who you are. You learned that you cannot build upon a lie or set foundations into shifting sands.

After accepting your truth you begin to live by your own code of moral ethical standards in equality with others and in harmony with the universe.

Now it is time to enter a phase of self healing and realise the importance of self love, giving yourself the required time and space to be able to breathe amid the chaos of life. Your inner voice has awakened and you can now hear its prophecies, visions, and dreams of the future. YOU create possibilities for yourself at the same time as putting those obstacles in front of you that bar the way to progression. These self created obstacles can always be removed by a change in perspective. How can you not be awed at the sight of the stars above you on a moonless night? It is in these moments of grace you can forget all of the cares and worries that amass day by day, and in that silent communion with the sky you can foster a deep connection with one or more of the constellations. You also feel a need to enhance and bring to life that star that shines within, and this feeling becomes more urgent.

> "Count de Gébelin considers the great star to be Sothis or Sirius; the other seven are the sacred planets of the ancients. He believes the female figure to be Isis in the act of causing the inundations of the Nile which accompanied the rising of the Dog Star."
>
> — Manly Palmer Hall, *Secret Teaching of All Ages*.

A star maiden takes many forms in our culture and if we consider for a moment the image on the Rider Waite Tarot card she leaves nothing to the imagination.

We see a naked female form pouring the essence of life (water) on to the ground and into the water beside her. In the background there is a barren landscape in which seven stars crown the head of the figure from behind in the sky.

Perched on a tree to the right of the figure is the image of a bird and not just any bird but an Ibis which is associated with

Thoth. The message here is that by following your own star and shining brightly for all to see, you can trust that you can reach your dreams and bring them to manifestation. Are we not in truth made from stardust? The essence of the teaching is that the future isn't certain but that there are always possibilities, with space for health, healing and rejuvenation. Freedom from oppression allows the inner self to fully awaken and see the light of hope in the darkness. To be inspired, create joy, experience lightness of being, peace and calm within; Isis Crowned with Sceptre in her role as wife, mother and teacher.

Questions

What gives you hope? Are you inspired by those around you or do you inspire others to reach for their dreams? Do you have a vision of your future and if so do you have the confidence to step into it now?

The Moon

You find yourself wandering a barren wasteland that is grey and dull and seemingly lifeless. The air around you seems stifled and cold and there is an oppressive atmosphere which makes it hard to see much of anything clearly in this place. As you look down at your feet there is a shining pathway, glowing dimly and which is illuminating a way forward that you can travel. You step on to this silvery shining path and almost immediately begin to feel lighter in being and your burdens are lifted momentarily. You walk slowly and deliberately through this landscape of darkness and shadows, where dimly lit shapes lurk in the peripheral of your vision. Amorphous forms wisp in and out of view.

Up ahead you can see two towers and you become aware of two guardians that come and join you at this point. They guide you through the space between the towers which is a strange and timeless portal and as you look up you see the bright orb of the full moon high above you in the sky. Around the edges of the moon there are subtle tones of a hazy indigo aura which radiates out into the dark skies. You keep going forward on the silvery path with your guardians close by. They lead you through to the other side of the moon and into the unknown.

Take a moment to experience the calm, peace and serenity that is here in this place. Allow images to arise and bubble to the surface. Watch and observe as shapes and forms rise up and morph into recognisable things. Long pause

There is no need to fear the unknown. Observe, be patient and know that there is calm, peace and stillness within the shadows of the mind. The more familiar you become with the journey to this place and of the knowing that this is where you can overcome fears, why not choose something now that needs to be brought out into the light and healed.

(Long Pause.)

In this place you have left behind you the ordinary world and have stepped temporarily into another dimension in your imagination and here you can be still and know the unknown. This is your bridge constructed by the High Priestess, so that you can travel back and forth as easily as you pass back and forth between waking and sleeping.

When you are ready return from this place and your guardians will escort you back to the landscape and path upon which you started your journey. Write down any insights that you may have had during this journey.

The Moon

On some of the traditional images for the Moon, you find a crayfish half in and half out of the water in a somewhat barren landscape. Stranded halfway between two towers or the pillars of Jachin and Boaz. On the Initiate's Way Moon there is a figure of a priestess standing in salutation, greeting the face of the goddess that you meet at the time of the full moon.

Will you or won't you descend into the depths of the unconscious and travel through the gateway into the unknown? It is a path which is lonely because it must be undertaken alone but it also heralds a time of cleansing and a release of trapped emotions and blockages, that may have up until now held you back in your quest to know yourself better. This presents a chance for you to calm extreme emotions, though caution may be required if you are of a sensitive nature. This is a time for sleep and rest requiring a period of withdrawal and introspection.

The tidal nature of emotions experienced during lunation's or monthly menstruation are no coincidence and women are no strangers to the rise and fall of moods, energy and our connection to those tides that govern the flow of the sea back and forth. Also the marked effect upon extra sensory perception and psychic sensitivity. One only has to visit the accident and emergency department of any hospital to experience the effect of the full moon first hand.

Vivid dreams, mystical experiences and a definite connection to the "otherworld" are themes to be explored during this part of the journey. Understanding the nature of the spiritual experience comes with an acceptance that one has to venture alone into the unknown, to face the fears or any other demons or monsters that

18. The Moon

may be lurking in the mind. The term lunacy can evoke terrifying visions of madness and behaviour that are otherwise deemed abnormal. Things that are just out of the normal range of sense perception like ghosts, attachments, unnatural disturbances and influences from the unseen. Places, people and energies in one's environment, these fall under the influential nature of the moon. The energy detected when standing under the light of the full moon is subtle but apparent, it can cause all kinds of hallucinations and strange occurrences in the psyche of an unbalanced individual. Almost as if the person's worst nightmares are coming to greet them in the waking world. There may be feelings that arise which have no bearing in reality, because they are the product of the imagination.

Think of those moments when you are just about to fall asleep and you experience fleeting images which drift in and out of recognition, this is hypnagogic imagery that could easily be mistaken for apparitions in the room or visitations of spirits. The liminal boundary, crossover point or transition between waking and sleeping is a strange place full of phantasms and disconnected thoughts, not quite reaching the deeper layers of memory and awareness, and not quite letting go of the perception of the physical world around us.

Depending on your standpoint the moon can be perceived as simply the reflected light of the Sun or as a portal and gateway into another realm entirely, whose light comes from another place. However you decide to look at it, you are on your own, as you set out to experience all that you have hidden from yourself by burying it in the shadows of the past. This needn't be an unpleasant journey for you as you can also understand yourself much better, as you engage with your fantasies of the imagination. As long as you realise that is all they are, a product of the imagination. Whether or not you are in control of the flow of information coming from the imagination, will be the governing factor of whether you are able to seek out the timeless mysteries here, or whether you will find yourself helplessly drowning in the flow of information.

At the time of the full moon there are instincts and urges that are primal in nature which surface and require attention, so that they don't cause disturbances to the health and psychic wellbeing. The stereotypical image of the werewolf howling at the moon portrays one of these outcomes, when the tide of the unconscious has taken a hold over the rational nature and the animal instincts are allowed rule. Where do we begin seeking wisdom if not through the path of the moon? Seeing through the illusions requires great courage and strength. Paying particular attention to dreams and if there is a need to sleep and rest, then do so for your healing requires space to breathe, feel and just 'be'. You can also employ ritual to aid brief respite from the toils and tribulations of life, delving into the world of fantasy and imagination through rites of passage or ritual enactments.

Unconquered Sun

Close your eyes and allow yourself to relax. Focus your energy and attention on your breathing and find a natural rhythm that suits you. As you become aware of the breath coming in and out of your lungs notice how each breath affects your body. When you breathe in are there any changes in your body? When you breathe out how does your body feel? Are there any sensations that you didn't notice until you began your rhythmic breathing? What about the spaces between each breath and are there any significant changes to your body during the pause between breaths? Take a moment to scan your body for any areas of tension. gently allowing them to release. *Short pause.*

Ask now that your spirit guides, ancestors and any guardians that you have encountered so far, journey with you in this next part of your awakening.

See yourself walking towards a garden gate. As you walk towards it the gate opens of its own accord and you walk through it into a beautiful garden full of roses of every colour and kind. The aroma of the blooms is really strong and you breathe deeply of the magnificent scent. You notice there is a wall surrounding the garden, and walking along the path, it takes you out of the garden of roses and leads you into another part of this beautiful place that has several trees. A sacred grove of trees in a circle.

You walk into the middle of the grove and find a bench almost hidden amongst the vines, flowers and greenery which have crept up around it.

Sit down for a moment on this bench and take in the beauty of the mature trees that have grown, since their caretaker created this magical space for reflection and introspection.

As you sit here fully present in the moment the sun comes out from behind the clouds, shining through the trees and it creates a warm glow just above the top of your head. Almost immediately the sunlight forms a big sphere of yellow light. See it there, feel it there, the radiating healing warmth pulsating at the crown of your head. The yellow ball of the sun begins to move down through the top of your head and travels down through the back of your neck and into your shoulders. Everything that this light touches radiates and pulsates with the vibration of the sun. It soothes and clears away any negativity that may have been lingering within you, as it moves down your spine and into your solar plexus. You feel energy gathering within your solar plexus chakra, swirling and pulsating with the creation and birthing of your inner sun. Concentrate on this yellow ball of energy at your solar plexus as it slowly begins to expand and radiate outwards to include the whole of your torso. As the energy grows it expands more and more until the whole of your being is contained within and you are radiating and pulsating as one with this creative light. Resonate within this healing energy for as long as you need to and release all of your fears, self limiting beliefs and negative thought patterns. Long pause.

The pulsating aura expands now outside of your body and any beings or spirits, or discarnate entities that may have found themselves attached to you, can move on now through this light and go on to find their next plane of evolvement.

(Short pause.)

Concentrates again on the light in your solar plexus as a beam of light comes from it and shines down through you, until it comes out through the soles of your feet and down into the earth. You are grounded, centred and fully present in your body.

You feel much lighter now, energised and revitalised by the light of your inner sun. The glow recedes but you are left with feelings of joy and anticipation for the rest of your journey.

Silently thank your guides and ancestors who travelled with you and walk back through the garden of roses along the path until you find the gate from which you came through. Slowly returning to normal waking consciousness, you become aware of your body, your feet on the floor, and after three you will be wide awake and in the room. 1,2,3. Wiggle your hands and toes and stretch your body.

Unconquered Sun

One of the ideas for you to consider here is that of your *inner sun* or the seat of your consciousness and the outer personality, or mask that you project out into the world joining together to create a new being. The freedom of movement for information to travel between the lunar side of our consciousness, or that which is hidden beneath the surface of your awareness, being brought out into the light so that as you connect to and can access raw information from the source of the solar creativity, energy, and life that is abundant in our physical sun, whose strength waxes and wanes during the agricultural year. If you look at spiritual enlightenment as an allegory of a seed that you have planted within yourself, there are times when it is beneficial to plant, nurture, grow and rest and half the battle is knowing which are the times for these!

On the Crowley *Book of Thoth* image of the Sun you see two children hand in hand, underneath a representation of the physical sun in the sky above them. On the Initiate's Way arcana there is a typical representation of the sun as a glowing sphere of light. Imagine that the sun is a point within a circle and that it is surrounded by the 12 Astrological signs of the Zodiac. Representing one cycle of the sun through each of the astrological signs which is the allegory of our journey as the solar hero. As was discussed earlier in the text the cycle of going within and passing through the gates of these archetypal images in the inner world, is part of the Tarot journey.

Some traditions go so far as having exercises that are performed physically in which the signs are acted out or held as yogic poses, to align with the 12 archetypal images of the Zodiac.

19. *Unconquered Sun*

This phase of enlightenment begins at Aries and ends in Pisces, or rather at the time of the Spring Equinox in the northern hemisphere during the awakening of the power of the sun as a personification of an endless and invincible being. They who rise and travel through the sky during spring and summer, who then die and are replaced anew at the Summer Solstice, (or replaced by a twin) They then begin the descent into the underworld at Cancer only to be born again during the longest night at the Winter Solstice. The idea here is that by becoming aligned with a solar hero or deity you put yourself subjectively on to this path. With the trajectory of going through each of the signs in turn and learning from each experience before moving on to the next. If you consider this outer journey of the sun as being interchangeable and coinciding with the rise and fall of the astral tides that fluctuate and change during a year. You cannot fail to notice that the celebrations falling within these key times are recognised in most religions, in one way or another, as the dying and reborn sun, or the dying and reborn god.

In light of the spiritual journey that you have embarked upon since you considered the Fool and took the first tentative steps on the journey inwards to awaken the archetypes within. You can now reflect and take stock of where you are in terms of enlightenment and realisation within yourself.

You have become fully integrated within your personality, awakened within yourself after having experienced the subjective states, and the associated experiences in the physical world, after taking part in all of the previous journeys. What you should have discovered by this point is that lightness of being, life, joy and happiness, can only come from within as you manifest your true nature out into the world, having reached a different place of being entirely from where you started.

Most come to this journey at the beginning with no knowledge of these inner worlds and or the experiences awaiting in these hidden realms.

When I was meditating within this part of the journey myself I was given the following to ponder;

S.O.L I.N.V.I.C.T.U.S

Invincible one, Unconquered Sun and Eternal being.

So consider briefly then that there is a part of you that does not die, but that travels through time waking and sleeping. It travels on and on during its timeless journey through experience after experience. If you are to reach a place of harmony on this journey, then at some point you must learn how to bring these dual aspects of your solar nature and your lunar nature together. In other words to merge your conscious and subconscious together so that they can act as a whole, rather than you constantly moving in and out of one state or the other.

In some decks like that of Crowley Thoth and the Rider-Waite Tarot there are two children in the garden, and they are shown underneath a representation of the sun and the two generative forces of masculine and feminine opposites.

Gemini is ruled by Mercury and the two children personify the serpents entwined around the *caduceus*. (Manly Palmer Hall, *Secret Teachings of the Ages*)

The heart and mind must function in harmony with each other for a balanced existence and until they do it is only natural that one or the other should lead. The twins standing in a garden is a perfect metaphor for these two states of being. Psychic wholeness and a fully awakened state is what you are aiming for at the conclusion of this stage in your journey.

Questions

What are your energy levels like, are you mostly energised or do you have periods of feeling depleted? How much time do you spend outside in nature? Would you say you are fully integrated into your personality, awake and aware?

Judgement

I want you to take a moment to close your eyes and relax. Focus your energy and attention on your breathing and take in a few nice deep breaths. With every breath your body feels more and more relaxed. Count to the steady count of four. In to the count of four and out to the count of four, continue this breathing until you have achieved perfect relaxation.

As you go deeper and deeper into yourself you see a vision appearing in your imagination. It's blurry at first but when it comes into focus you see behind your eyes the radiance of the orange and red of a blazing sunrise. You immerse yourself in these flame colours and almost at once your body begins to glow with the warmth that you would expect to feel coming from an open fire. Your whole body radiates with this sensual warm orange glow and you slowly realise that you have a fine brittle shell around you. You are in the embryonic centre of the orphic egg out of which you are almost ready to hatch. You feel energy radiating from within and all around you. The pulse of the universe resonates throughout your entire being. Are you ready to radiate outwards from the central core of this ball of flame? Everything you have ever done in this lifetime flashes in front of you in a succession of images from birth up until this moment in time. Pause here.

You pause and reflect momentarily upon what you have achieved so far in your life.

Set the intentions now for your future and raise your serpent from within, until you cannot contain it any longer and it takes on a life of its own. You feel a great surge of energy and as it courses throughout your entire being, the shell cracks open and obliterates into thousands of tiny fragments. The dust from the explosion emanates out into the space around you and you feel a previously unknown sense of freedom as you are no longer restricted or contained anymore.

Above you is the midnight blue of the night sky studded with the tiny pinpoints of the lights of a thousand stars. As your attention expands up into the sky you sense movement. Tiny shooting stars streak across the sky in silent communion with the open space above you. The deep velvet midnight blue brings your awareness into your forehead, to the space just between your eyes where there is a violet glow. You watch for a moment as sparks of violet, indigo and blue flicker as the light of the stars gives birth to something in your imagination. Pause here.

You feel a tickling sensation in your pineal gland as it is cleansed of any impurities that may have been clogging it and a snakelike serpentine energy moves out of your third eye, and travels around each side of your forehead and this living energy creates a radiant crown all the way around your skull. An inviting silence pervades and you enter into a blissful peace and union with all of eternity.

You feel yourself being lifted up, your subtle bodies merge together into one and this state of union or bliss, within your self, emits a ray of light. Like a beacon out into the ether, in an explosion of light that comes from deep within your core.

Feel this incredible light shining from you, with you, connecting you with every single living thing in existence. Look down at your feet and you see that you are hovering above a shining path, and it is so bright that your *eyes hurt to look at it. Bring yourself into alignment with your path and set yourself on it so that you can walk easily along it. Travel along this road as far as it takes you and when you are ready come back to waking consciousness and record your experience in your journal.*

20. Judgement Call

Judgement Call

On this Initiate's Way arcana you see the Gates of Dawn behind which lies a shining path awaiting you as a seeker of the mysteries. It is a road that is presented as a choice after hearing the call from spirit, and to walk on a path of service to others. Here is a crossroads and there is no turning back from this point, so the outcomes will be very much dependant on how you make your choice, with your head or your heart, or both? In the Rider Waite Judgement trump we see the dead rising from open graves, this signifies an awakening from a dead life into one of purpose and meaning. It is associated with a calling, or hearing a call to fully embrace life. Inner knowing and following your own path, recognising synchronicity and acting on it, these things can lead you into a life full of rich experiences, vigour, vitality and passion. If you choose to walk a path of morality and valour, and consciously enter into service towards humanity the rewards outweigh any sacrifices that you may have to make in order to do this.

At this point in the spiritual journey you will by now have become adept at building up mental images and exploring the realms of the imagination behind these timeless doorways. Take a moment now to recap where you have travelled, what you have learned and the process by which you have discovered the right way, direction and which path is yours to walk. Time has its constraints and there is only a limited amount of it in this one lifetime.

If you choose now to dedicate it to a higher purpose, the positive goals can bring great change, not only do you bring positive change into your own life but you also affect the lives of those you help along the way. Once you bring your inner and outer worlds into alignment and proceed forward with balance and harmony between thoughts, imagination, emotional and physical wellbeing, look for the hidden observer. See things with greater clarity and awareness, trust your instincts and insight. And as you move through the rest of your existence on this physical place, use these inner resources, wisdom and knowledge that you have gained access to during this journey of enlightenment. These landscapes within bring the magic of it all out into the world around you.

In the previous image of the Sun you burned away the illusionary veil that separates the inner from the outer. Feel the harmony and union with the natural world and the deep connection to every living thing. You have touched something sacred and experienced a different way of being, in another mode of consciousness. So that now you can completely let go of any feelings of separation or isolation that you may have had, as you come out of your shell to embrace life. The term resurrection after judgement can imply all manner of symbolisms that could easily be misconstrued. But if you think about it in terms of the calling being a process, by using this process you can understand existence, not just concerning things that happen in your own life, but from a perspective where you understand your place in the world, and how you can take part in working towards the evolution of humanity.

By immersing yourself fully in the fluctuations of the life force of the planet you become more sensitive to things on a different level. You may begin to feel the peaks and troughs of change to political structures before they happen, and become attuned to the lines of force which move behind the scenes, at times of great change or conflict in the human consciousness.

Everyone is at different levels of learning but collectively we all go through stages and cycles and this for you will possibly bring one of realisation. That something now is coming to an end and that it is making way for the birthing, or the beginning of something completely new. The birthing is that of your new life, it is manifesting in the world around you. It is blossoming with every new connection that you make, in every act of kindness without thought for self. It is reaching a mature perspective which then realises that growth is a necessity on every level, personal, spiritual, physical, mental and collectively as a species. The physical world is not all that there is and that the path of enlightenment and spirituality can result in liberation.

You stand at the threshold of a greater understanding. Finding a centre in relation to your place in life and understanding your roles, begins with the process of embracing your true self. Not the projections and masks that you wear to disguise your fears and hide your true nature but that essence of your core that shines and radiates out into the world, unashamed and stable. Supporting and caring, loving and being loved without regard for social status or personal gain.

Most of us at one point in our lives has experienced feelings of being lost or disconnected from those around us. The experience of a separate-ness that divides us from those close, and creates an illusory sense of being alone in the world. Overcoming fears of this kind and coming to independent conclusions about the true meaning of life and existence is important, but the essence of the lesson to learn is that you can never truly be free while others around you are suffering. That answering the call is consciously choosing to help others to move forward for their healing, assisting others to attain some kind of relief from their fears and suffering from a place of unconditional love.

Recognising that the dormant potential within can be awakened for greater achievements. During this time of realisation it may be that you are presented with an opportunity, a once in a lifetime chance to do something extraordinary. Call it an awakening from within or being guided, however you look at it after this experience you will not be the same person that you were. With greater clarity comes inner strength, which allows for more productivity and creativity to flow freely without restriction. Putting fear out of the equation and trusting that you are doing what you are meant to be and looking to the universe for signs and coincidences to show that are on the right path. Certain people will be drawn to you and they will be integral to the next phase in your journey. You will be walking alongside others who resonate on the same frequency, working from the same ideals or moral values. Removals of any limitations that you have placed on your development and having the courage to stand up and do what is in your heart.

You may experience a surge in interest in certain areas of study and knowledge being presented to you, in a way that allows you to uncover secrets and bring out latent knowledge, wisdom and abilities in you to ground them into your own work. It is vitally important to be open and honest in all of your intentions and to share your visions with those who are drawn towards you. Others who are seeking from a place of morals and ethical perspectives, they are your comrades at arms and co-creators of a new world.

Whether it is as simple as breaking the mould and stepping out and doing something in a different way, or creating a new venture from the ground and building it into something that flourishes and benefits the lives of those in your community. Be assured that your purpose and meaning will begin to show itself to you in a crystal clear vision and you can set out to do your best at whatever those intentions may be. There will be communication at all levels, cooperation and friendships, allies and networking that brings highly skilled people together to create, create, create! Through the word, deed, thought and actions.

Questions

Do you know why you are here and your reasons for being? Have you noticed an increase in synchronistic events and a nagging that just won't go away about something that you are supposed to do? Are you ready to awaken from a sleeplike state, to serve your purpose here and now?

You are about to embark on your final journey through the Archetypes of the Tarot. You have learned so much and yet only scratched the surface of what is available to use as resources if you only know where to look. Deep mysteries await at this time and you are going on a journey to seek a hidden place that few have managed to discover, or have given up along the way because the way became too difficult.

The World – World Serpent – Universe

You are walking through craggy mountains high up in a remote and deserted place. The birds reel overhead and their cries ricochet off the faces of the mountains. The sky is clear blue with the tiniest wisps of clouds and the heat from the sun is making you feel tired now. The road in front of you has been less travelled there are thorny thickets invading with every step you take, and the grass either side of the path rustles as it sways in the wind.

You have a staff with you and begin to move some of the more invasive branches out of the way. You know you should stay on this path as this is where your guide told you that you must travel until you reach the fork in the road. It gets harder and harder with each step but you press on until you see a crossroads up ahead. The road disappears completely from underneath your feet but you can sense that the crossroads is not far from this point. The thorns and branches seem to tighten as you try to go forward from here. Trust your intuition. Ask for your guides to step forward now and lead you through this part of your journey.

For a moment you see swirling colours, a rainbow mist that spirals out in all directions. You wait a moment until the swirling colours have receded and to your amazement you stand at the entrance of a wide tree lined path that goes far away from you into the distance. You are standing underneath two tall trees with roots that are nearly bigger than you, these are bent together at the top to form an archway.

The roots look like giant gnarled fingers and they disappear into the ground below. Imagine how far down these roots must go ,bearing in mind how tall the trees are. You hear someone whisper your name from a little way down the path in front of you and you walk through this gigantic tree archway and onto a tree lined avenue. You hear the murmuring of insects in the forest and the dappled sunlight creates patterns on the ground as you walk. You feel as if you are being drawn somewhere special and as you go further into the forest along this avenue of ancient trees, you see something a little way off in the distance.

There is a patch of open sky and the sun is illuminating a structure of some sort in the centre of a clearing. As you get closer you see that it is some kind of step pyramid. The stone is roughly cut on the wall that is facing you and there are seven hewn steps that lead up to a stony face of the goddess. The steps end at her closed mouth and you take a moment to see all the detail that has been carved into this monument. Walk around the building and see what else you can find on the outside. Are there any more carvings? Can you see a doorway? *Pause here.*

You are joined now by a guide who tells you that to gain entry you must offer something to the goddess. What are you willing to give in order to progress further on your spiritual journey? Take a moment to ask yourself what has brought you to this sacred place? Do you have any questions? Ask your companion about any questions that you might have now. *Pause here.*

You find yourself within a large circular stone atrium. The blue sky above you is cloudless and the air feels warm. Sunlight illuminates the centre of the structure and you notice on the floor there are four carved figures representing the four fixed signs of the zodiac. The walls are also carved in bas relief and you recognise the poses of the rest of the signs of the zodiac who are engaged in portraying a story all around the inner of the circular wall. You walk around looking at each in turn. Pay attention to any information that you are given and if you feel drawn more to any particular sign engage in conversation with the image and ask if there is anything that you need to know for you to proceed on your spiritual quest. *Long Pause Here.*

As the sun begins to dip and disappears behind the craggy mountains in the distance, the atrium takes on a completely different atmosphere. The sky darkens and one by one the stars emerge as the dusky pink haze of sunset, quickly turns into an inky midnight blue sky studded with thousands of stars. This place allows you to attune yourself with the passage of time and you feel the magic of your ancestors stirring within you.

You are the product of thousands of lifetimes, and those who have gone before you. Take a moment to appreciate everything that you have and the gifts that you have been blessed with in this life, before considering making your return journey back to your current incarnation. The sky above you morphs into the distant memory, a recollection of the stars as they were positioned the day you were born into this life. You feel inspired and renewed *with hope and optimism for the future and you say your silent farewell to this magical place.*

The vision of the atrium slowly fades and you find yourself standing once again at the crossroads where you started your journey. As you walk back through the craggy mountains with the sun shining down on you, you bring back everything that you have experienced. Make sure you are fully present and back in the room by clapping your hands or stamping your feet.

Write down or discuss with any journeying companions anything significant that you experienced during your journey.

The World (Change and Transition phase)

(Saturn/Earth/Cyclical Time) This is the conclusion of a long journey and the beginning of a new cycle, of feeling empowered, moving past previously stressful situations, and of the celebration of your gifts and talents. Recognition for hard work, achievements and change for the better; Initiations.

On the Initiate's Way World Image you see a central figure standing within a laurel wreath, and with the pillars of Jaoqin and Boaz behind her. Above and below her she is encircled by a green serpent depicting the higher and lower realms. She walks through the flames with no fear, or doubt, and she can move in and out of the different worlds as easily as waking and sleeping. With four fixed signs of the zodiac, after integrating the wisdom of the higher self, and after having conquered the animal passions of the lower realms, this figure is a treading a different path.

One of the key factors at this stage in the development process, is that of growth and recognition. Of just how far you have come since the outset of your initial first footing on to the fool's journey into the unknown. Long cycles are coming to a conclusion and there will be some kind of reward for the process. Whether that is a new outlook and perspective, or simply the satisfaction of doing something to the best of your ability and standing back to take a moment to enjoy the feeling of a job well done before setting off on another long journey.

21. *The World / World Serpent / Universe*

Important life events and rites of passage are depicted here and the emphasis is on changing things for the better by recognising the need for working on one's self and making lasting internal changes.

In the Crowley/Lady Frieda Harris image for this trump we see the four fixed signs of the Zodiac in the four corners of the card. They can be attributed to the four elemental guardians of Earth, Air, Fire and Water. The central figure dances with one foot on a snake and the other raised, and she is pointing to the motion of the source of light that is coming from the opened eye in the top corner, which is emitting light. In her other hand she is holding a crescent shaped instrument which could be one of the hands of time from a clock face. Surrounding her are the constellations through which she moves and dances as time passes, where ages begin, flourish and fade. Continuity of existence is one of the themes presented here, as is a universal state of being, and a perspective that has broken outside of the normal realms of everyday living.

"End, beginning, it's all the same. Big Change." – Zelda from the *Dark Crystal*

In the Rider-Waite/Pamela Coleman Smith version of this image there is a lady dancing in the centre of the card and she has a scarf that billows around her in the wind. Her legs form the symbol for the Hebrew letter Kaph. She is holding a wand in each hand and her left leg crosses the other to form the symbol for Sulphur. She is enclosed within a wreath symbolising the centre of the vesica piscis, or the place within which worlds merge and you can access the timeless wisdom and knowledge.

Again you find the four characters portraying the four fixed signs of the Zodiac; the four worlds that we associate with the four suits of the Minor Arcana. The positioning in the centre of a wreath suggests that it is within nature that you will find your answers to any questions about the mysteries.

Manly Palmer Hall speaks of the figure as representing the "divine fire and the heart of the Great Mystery" and the elemental worlds in which we experience our lives." By entering into a journey of discovery as you have been by traveling through these archetypes of the Tarot, will have brought you closer to understanding the true nature of things and hopefully will have set you on a path to finding a course for the rest of your life. So that you can fulfil your potential and do what you came here to do.

Forgetting your path and purpose happens amid the distractions and chaos of life, but if you must make time every now and again to regain your sense of direction, to reorient and remind yourself of the bigger picture of where you are going and why. Then you will never stray too far from the path. There is much inner work to be done before anyone can consider themselves enlightened in any way and the process of learning never ends. You are given life lessons and you should then assimilate what you have learned, so that you don't repeat the same mistakes in the future.

Consideration and understanding of the cyclic process of astrology and the signs of the zodiac, and its important relationship with the wheel of the year, should be experienced and studied in great detail to allow progression of the soul in its journey towards wholeness.

Spiritual alchemy is not for the fainthearted and comes with its own set of rewards that are priceless. One of these being the inner world and the outer world coming together into alignment and harmony with each other, and experiencing the world tree as the centre point of being. The finding of ones place or centre within the world is the aim of the inner journey for this archetype.

If you can stay centred then your place in the world becomes clearer and the journey through this life becomes very different to that of eternally seeking without and never finding. Becoming grounded or putting down your spiritual roots is essential. Settling on a path that is going to be conductive and productive, creative and harmonious with the world around you, allows you to exist in union with the forces that weave and dance the universal dance of existence.

Jade Melany

www.initiatesway.co.uk
www.esoteric-art.co.uk
info@esoteric-art.co.uk

Richard Abbot

The Hermitage Development Centre, Established 1983
TAROT & NUMEROLOGY / PSYCHIC HEALING / SPIRITUAL PROGRESS / PSYCHIC GROWTH / MYSTICAL AWARENESS / PERSONAL DEVELOPMENT / KARMA & PAST LIVES / THE INNER REALMS

www.thehermitage.org.uk
answers@yourwayforward.co.uk

Caitlín Matthews

Caitlín Matthews teaches divination internationally. She is the author of over 70 books including *Untold Tarot: The Lost Art of Reading Ancient Tarots*, Complete Lenormand Oracle Handbook, The Celtic Book of the Dead and, with John Matthews, the classic best-selling Tarot, *Complete Arthurian Tarot*, as well as four other Tarots. She studies early small-card oracles and is responsible for the republication of two original mid-19th century Lenormand decks: the Belgium *Daveluy* and the Austrian *Zauberkarten*,

See www.hallowquest.org.uk. Also, follow her divination and myth blog on http://caitlin-matthews.blogspot.co.uk/

How to read Tarot for yourself and others

Laying out cards

The process of reading Tarot is simple. Anyone can do it if they put their mind to it. Shuffle the cards while thinking about a question that you require some guidance on. When it feels right stop shuffling and lay three cards face down in front of you. Do this by putting one central card down first and then put one either side of that. Put them so that the images of the Tarot cards are facing you and not the backs. This is your "present moment"

Then deal twelve cards around the outside of these, starting on the top right. Put one card on the top right and then one card on the top left, one card on the bottom left and then one card on the bottom right. Repeat this process another two times until you have a layout that has three cards in the middle, three cards top right of these, three cards top left of these, three cards bottom left and three cards bottoms right.

This is what is known as the Golden Dawn spread and I have used this to read cards for myself and others for over 25 years. If you already use Tarot and have a favourite spread then use whichever works for you. With your question in mind find the meanings for the first three cards presented in this book and read the interpretations.

Consider how they are relevant, or not, to your situation. Study the relationship between the cards grouped together. Are they positive or negative. What do the images on the cards say to you? Do they evoke any feelings?

Then move on to the top right three cards. This is your future path should you choose it. Look up the interpretations in the book and consider the relationship between these three cards. Are there any connections that jump out at you? Think about your question and notice how you feel. Then move on to the top left three cards. These are other influences and things for you to consider about your future path. Try to get a bird's eye view of the situation by reading these interpretations and perhaps write down any thoughts of feelings that arise during the process of reading.

When you have spent a little time with the top row, then move on to the three cards on the bottom left of the central cards. These three cards are the influences coming in and changes to watch out for, things to expect. Perhaps these influences have already started to come in. This is what to expect from your current path.

The last three cards on the bottom right are external influences affecting your situation, in your home, work, family, people around you etc. Con- sider anything that is having a direct influence on you in the interpretations. How do you feel about this? Are there changes that you could make based upon the interpretations?

Remember you have choices about everything in life and sometimes it can be as simple as the fact that you have not made a decision about what you really want, because you are apprehensive of what the outcome might be! Once you have clear idea of what you want, you can then start to make steps towards it. After reading the interpretations and getting a higher perspective sometimes it makes decision making easier, as emotions often cloud judgement and make it difficult to see things clearly.

Reading Tarot can help to gain that clarity of perspective which is needed.

Using Tarot cards to read for others

In my 25 years of using and reading with the Tarot the most frequent question I am asked is concerning relationships. Even though I always advise that decisions within relationships ultimately lie with them, the client still always want to know more about where the other person stands, what they are thinking, how the other person perceives them etc.

Setting out cards to read for other people I have found that the two spreads which are the most effective are either the 15 Card Golden Dawn spread which we have discussed already or the Celtic Cross spread.

The simplest method for beginners to use as they get used to the cards and reading for themselves and others is a three card spread which gives one card each for past, present and future.

2 Past 1 Present 3 Future

Lay these out side by side

This can later be extended into the Golden Dawn Spread once you get more comfortable with the cards and their meaning. If you are going to use the Celtic Cross Spread it is a good idea to familiarise yourself first with the court cards so that you can choose the right card to represent the person you are reading for before shuffling cards.

See the section on Court Cards which should help you decide which significator is the right one for the person depending on their characteristics. If you search on the internet you will find a diagram for the celtic cross which shows you where to place the cards.

A word on reversed meanings. As you get more confident with the cards you might like to introduce reversed cards. What this means is that during the shuffling you turn some of the cards upside down so that when you lay cards you may get some that are reversed.

It doesn't always mean that the card will be negative in its interpretation, but I have found that it can add an extra dimension to the reading and gives more insight. You don't have to use reversed cards in your readings but I have presented them here for those that would like to use them.

Major Arcana interpretations

Fool

Throwing caution to the wind and acting without thinking. There is a wish to be carefree and tread a new path. Unconventional approach to solving problems within relationships. There is a sense of euphoria and being carried along by life rather than being in control. Risky ventures which re- quire a leap of faith. The unknown and all of its implications. Living in the present moment regardless of any concerns for the future or the past. Emotional overload such as when falling in love and ones senses are temporarily overwhelmed. Instant gratification. A new beginning in some area of life, out with the old and in with the new. Depending on circumstances it may be a new job, way of life, new lover etc but there is always the reminder you to look before you leap!

Reversed meaning

Avoidance of commitment and mania. Acting in a manner that does not suit the situation. Unaware that one's actions are having a detrimental effect on others.

Ignorance towards others and careless attitude towards sex. Impatience and unreliability towards those close. Unresolved issues being ignored. Wanting to escape from a situation rather than face up to responsibilities. Immaturity in love. Obsessive behaviour and infatuation.

Magician – Messenger

Stepping out of an ordinary situation and through sheer determination and willpower creating something new whether that be a new business opportunity or taking responsibility for your own future. There is a realisation or epiphany that having faith in ones own abilities and relying on inner resources will achieve desired results with effort and concentration of willpower. Very confident person.

Using the imagination to come up with solutions to problems. Creative thinking. Dynamic individual who communicates well with others. Clarity of thought, perception and ability to act on ideas and create something from those ideas. Willpower to see things through to completion. If there has been something on the mind that requires action then it is now time to focus and begin acting upon those thoughts. No time to waste!

Reversed meaning

Blockages, stagnation of thought. Someone or something getting in the way of the ability to move forwards. More often than not the querent's own attitude is causing the problem whether they realise it or not. Selfish tendencies and a refusal to consider how actions affect others. Manipulation of others for personal gain and misuse of power. Non productive relationship which is one sided and waste of energy for one person.

High Priestess

Listening to dreams and inner guidance for answers to questions. Intuition over reason. Feminine mysteries are implied here and the meeting of like minds. Seeking out instruction or spiritual counsel from knowledgeable sources. Going within. Inner knowing and doing what feels right rather than what what is expected. Unconventional solutions to difficulties are required. Cathartic processes and seeking inner worlds. Creating a sacred space in which to reflect. Inner knowing and prophetic states come easily, knowing when to act because there is are strong feelings.

Reverse meaning
Not listening to inner voice. Ignoring warning dreams or instincts. Out of touch with one's intuitive senses. Misunderstanding and misinterpreting situations. Confusion and unresolved mental and emotional blockages causing issues in the personality, which can cause relationship difficulties as the person may be acting out of character because the subconscious mind is overwhelming the conscious thought processes. Depression and fatigue. Chronic illnesses, and psychosomatic symptoms.

Goddess of the Grove – Empress

This card indicates a happy home where the querent is loved and gives freely of their love. Balanced relationships. Abundance. Love. A stable environment. Family. Child rearing and all aspects of mother- hood. Fulfilment in all areas of life. Care and consideration towards others, deep feelings and close friendships.

Creating a welcoming environment where friends and family alike feel at home. Living in the present moment with little regard for the past and not over- ly concerned with the future. Shared goals and common ground. Deep connection with nature.

Reversed Meaning
Difficulties in the home life, disturbances and lack of communication. Feeling uncomfortable in oneself and around

others. Isolation and withdrawal from close personal relationships. Maternal maladies. Conception difficulties and menstrual problems. Inability to cope with strong emotions. Disappointments in love. Negative behaviour. Stagnation within relationships and a refusal to accept other people as being just as important as self. Lack and loss. Infertility or unwanted pregnancies. self gratification instead of love.

God of the Grove – Emperor

Masculinity and power. Rules and regulations. Male oriented institutions. Outward or projected personality. Fathers influence. Mature, responsible and respected men. Domestic Routines. Too much reliance on order and routine. No spontaneity. It is not a good card for close personal relationships. Lack of confidence and self doubt create a negative attitude towards oneself and others.

Too much focus on the future to the detriment of the present moment. Energy is being directed towards other pursuits rather than relationships. Would rather lead than be equal in a partnership.

Reversed Meaning
Hidden feelings and no self expression. Resistance or dislike of authority figures. Circumstances are causing querent to feel inhibited, worthless and lacking. Not being given the chance for full potential to mature. For a woman if this card turns up in a reading reversed it may signify a man who has a negative attitude towards women and is more concerned with his own gratification.

In a reading for a male it shows he is less interested in showing affection, but rather demonstrating his power and sexual prowess.

Shaman – Heirophant

The appearance of this card in a reading suggests the need for counsel of some kind, whether religious or spiritual to assist in dealing with heavy burdens. Inner teacher stepping out. Support and guidance should be sought out from qualified professionals whether this is doctors, nurses, therapists, psychologists or a marriage guidance counsellor. The querent requires advice before any action can be taken when deal- ing with a problem. Endurance and strength within close personal relationships. Perhaps one person is guiding the other through emotional turmoil and both will learn a lot from the experience.

Reversed meaning

Highlighting a need to be creative when problem solving and seek out alternative methods rather than conventional routes for assistance. Seeking out ones own counsel and learn to listen to intuition on how to fix issues. Lifestyle choices may leave a lot to be desired and may create re- percussions in home life and social environment. Kidding ones self that everything is ok when in actual fact help is required to get back on track.

Difficulty accepting authority figures and distaste for order, preferring to be surrounded by chaos and confusion in life.

Lovers

In some readings this card presents a choice to be made between two lovers, and that there can be no turning back or changing ones mind once the decision has been made. Or it may be that there are two different courses of action that could be taken. Questions regarding long term commitment may be given a positive outcome should the card be in its upright position. Duality becoming singular or acting as one. Union within the self creating a whole personality. Definite change and progression and moving forward in life. Communication in all of its forms. Words, thoughts, actions, messages, movement.Communication.

Reversed Meaning
Avoidance of responsibility and reluctance to make a choice. Inaction and sitting on the fence. Taking the path of least resistance regardless of facts. Clouded judgement with perhaps an unwillingness to see things as they truly are. Attachment to the past rather than making decisions to affect the future. There may be a need to disengage emotionally and look without pre-conceived notions at all of the facts at hand and then bravely make choices for the future. Are there things that have been deliberately ignored and left to fester?

Chariot of the Moon

Home life, domestic issues and relationships with others are in the limelight now. There may be a choice about a long term commitment. Mothers roles. Tough choices and facing up to the truth of the situation and being pre- pared for the consequences of ones actions. A pivotal point of no return. Getting into the driving seat of your life. In some readings it can indicate a need to look at the reasons why certain things have happened in relationships, are there attachment issues that are restricting one or both parties from progressing in life? Clouded judgement and perhaps an inability to see clearly the effect of ones actions, and perceiving a one sided view of a relationship. There will generally be two sides to every story so perhaps it is time to consider how your actions affect others in relationships. Movement, travel, heritage, family lines and ancestry.

Reversed meaning
Upsets to family life are coming to an end. Problems are being solved and balance is returning. There may be lack of commitment or desire to connect with close personal relationships. Distraction in the home environment have caused the querent to miss out on significant opportunities. Disappointment at the actions of others and feeling let down. Watch out for things being deliberately sabotaged. Seeing the error of ones own ways and doing something to change it, to rectify actions that have been questionable. Breaking free from restrictive situations. Someone has been reluctant to make any lasting emotional connections or has kept true feelings hidden. Serious consideration of where and with whom the querent wishes to spend their future.

Fortitude (Strength) by Caitlin Matthews

Fortitude. Courage. Energy. Potential unchained. Confidence in action. Resolute defiance. Challenging what is commonly accepted. Tireless efforts. The appetite to live life. Drawing on deep resources.

Reversed Meaning
Weakness. Vacillation. Dispiritedness. Indifference. Succumbing to prevailing influences. Failure of nerve. Blind to your own power. Unable to access your potential. Unused gifts that fester.

Hermit

Avoidance of social interaction and choosing to be alone for whatever reason. Silence. Retreat. Introspection. Turning focus away from relationships to work on one's own wellbeing and spiritual subject matter rather than that of the mundane world.

There is a need to step back from the situation and ponder true feelings. Get your answers from within and do not make any decisions while under anyone else's influence, and make sure your own needs are being met within any relationships.

Reversed meaning
Spending too much time alone and losing objectivity. Feeling sorry for ones self and wallowing in self pity which is detrimental to the situation at hand.

There may be resistance to change and a negative attitude that has developed which needs to be curtailed. Be a little less closed minded and leave behind any attitudes that don't serve you anymore. Loneliness and a yearning for a close personal relationship. There is a positive aspect to this card reversed in that it means you are ready to come out of the spiritual darkness.

Wheel of Fortune

Things that have happened in the past may come up to be processed, and better opportunities begin to present themselves. Karma. Past life issues. In relationships it indicates better communications and seeing things more clearly. Reversals of bad luck and misfortune. Chance meetings and fate bringing new people into the foray. Being given the opportunity to make right any actions from the past that have had negative consequences. Fate. Destiny. Present moment. Staying centred in the now. Releasing trauma and blocks.

Reversed meaning Sudden misfortune and inexplicable events as things go awry. Seemingly bad luck and unplanned changes all happening all at once. Feelings of being tested and fighting destiny. Reasons for disruption may never be understood but whatever crisis are presented you are being given a chance to do the right thing. Things may be out of control temporarily but it isn't forever. Cyclical phase. Lessons that have not been learned are repeating.

Justice

This can mean that the querent can expect some dealings with Courts of Law or official persons to resolve matters. Solving disputes in a fair and rational manner and calm, clear thinking is required. Possibly there is need of intervention of a third party to mediate and restore balance once again. This card may also signify relationship breakdown and unfair behaviour towards either party. Parting of the ways in business or close personal relationships that require dividing of property, good or finances. Weighing of the heart and receiving fair outcome depending on actions.

Reversed meaning
No recognition from a partner as being an equal. For whatever reason there is an unwillingness to speak one's mind and be honest. A great deal of suffering as a direct result of past decisions and resulting consequences. Worst case scenario there may be unpleasant legal proceedings ahead. Too much attention being paid to the other in a partnership and losing faith in ones own abilities. Unfair and unjust behaviour by one or both parties. Balance required. Clarity and logical analysis of the situation.

Drowned/Hanged Man

Being prepared to give up the pursuit of wealth or status in order to achieve happiness and peace. Wilful submission in close personal relationships. Expectations. Sacrificing something for the greater good. Mystical states and deep connections. A different viewpoint may mean that the person who the reading is for appears foolish to those around him/her but in fact they have greater clarity or understanding. Revealing personal truth. Possible acceptance and commitment to a long term relationship/partnership. A foot in both the physical world and the world of spirit. Altruism.

Reversed meaning
When the card is reversed there is unease and spiritual vacuity. The querent has emotional problems and cannot relate well with others. There is a lack of emotional maturity and refusal to work on the inner needs, preferring instead to give everything to others and leave nothing for one's self. Denying strong feelings and emotions and giving in to negative thinking. Even though there have been significant achievements in life they seem unimportant and the querent needs to do some serious soul searching. Deep seated insecurities and confusion. Uncertain of place in the world.

Death/Transformation

Major changes in life. Initiations and rites of passage. Endings and beginnings. Personality destruction and rebirth. Choices that can ultimately bring happiness after a period of sadness. Moving on from unpleasant experiences and cutting oneself off from anything in the past that may have caused unhappiness, sorrow or pain. Letting go. Responsibility for self. Period of unpleasant or uncomfortable circumstances before turning a corner and beginning again. Stepping out and creating a new life adventure, moving to a new place, getting a new job, changing career are all the kinds of things that are associated with this card in a reading.

Reversed meaning
Fighting against change. Inability to see things clearly causes unnecessary discomfort. Experiences are overwhelming when the card is reversed. The querent finds it hard to see the light at the end of the tunnel preferring instead to be stubborn and resist. Reluctance to accept the difficulties within a relationship and address what needs to be done. Inability to adapt to necessary change means the situation will be much harder than it needed to be. Refusal to see what the best course of action is has made things much more difficult to bear. Lessons unlearned. Obstinate behaviour. Negative thinking. Depression and anxiety over future.

The Art of Temperance

When this card turns up in a reading the person it represents has the capacity to deal with situations in a calm, clear and focussed manner. Balanced and stable individuals, even tempered and competent at making their own decisions, acting from a rational frame of mind. Do not make any rash decisions. Take time to look at everything carefully and maintain balance at all times. Resist any urges to act on impulse. The beginning of a period of rebirth. Inner work. Meditation. Self analysis and getting in touch with one's authentic or true self. Higher genius. Creation of a new way of being.

Reversed meaning
Conflict and imbalance. Inability to see things clearly. Too many things are cluttering the mind and decisions cannot be made because of feelings of being overwhelmed. Restlessness and tension causing anxiety and fatigue. Bouncing about from one situation to another without resolution. Not thinking before

speaking or acting which has far reaching consequences. Not being able to share and be open with those close. Behaving in a way that is just not appropriate for the situation.

Distractions and mania. Lack of insight and understanding of needs.

Pan – Hermes – Devil

Frustration at restrictions and life circumstances which appear to be out of one's control. Oppression and stifling situations which seem to have no end in sight. Emotions overruling intellect. Passions and obsessive behaviour that require healing. Personality issues. Feelings of being trapped and bound. Weight of problems making life unbearable until the need for change is accepted. Find or create one's own way in life rather than succumb to the pressure to conform. Finances, material world and concerns, self reliance and grounding of ideas into physical manifestations.

Reversed meaning

Things have gone on for too long and problems have become unbearable. Breaking point has been reached and things cannot continue as they have been. Long term solutions required and problem solving to turn things around for the better. Uncomfortable situations have forced actions that should have been instigated a long time ago. Heading into an awakening and dealing with aspects of personality which were hidden and dormant until the point of no return is been reached. Parting of the ways. Temporary separations. Absence of love, or abnormal desires which may require therapy.

The Tower

Breaking down of illusions and revealing personality traits and masks. Uncovering the true nature of the self. Misfortune and disruption in life events. Learning hard life lessons. Trauma, distress, and sudden shocks to the system that bring about a different perception. In relationships it can signify a change in how one views their partner as a result of discovering something previously unknown. Extreme disappointment, emotional discomfort and uncomfortable revelations. Being tested and scrutinized by others for ones actions and behaviour. Being tested and scrutinized by others for ones actions and behaviour. Viewed from the point of view as a blessing in disguise often the events that at the time may seem awful turn out to have been for reasons that we were unaware of, and allow significant growth and development as a result. Breaking down of unrealistic self - images.

Reversed meaning

The tower of destruction has still fallen but it may not have such a devastating effect as the card appearing in a reading the right way up. Less severe revelations and perhaps being able to avoid future disasters by learning form ones mistakes and recognising and correcting destructive patterns. Mild depression as one realises that hopes and dreams have been crushed or not brought to fruition as was previously expected.

Unrealistic expectations and fooling ones self so as to avoid confronting inner fears and self destructive pat- terns. Wearing rose tinted spectacles.

The Star Sothis

Serenity and peaceful states of being. Feelings of being connected to others and seeing things clearly. Altruistic personalities. Mystical states of awareness and inspiration that comes from the pursuit of Spirituality. Healing and places that we go for rest, respite and sanctuary so that we can regather our energies to deal with the harder times in life. Creating sacred spaces. Cleansing and retreating into meditative states of being. Receiving guidance and wisdom from otherworldly sources. Joy. Hope. Rest and recovery after difficulties. Blessings that come when least expected. Within close personal relationships it can suggest a renewed bond within an established partner- ship, or a new relationship. Reaching out to meet new friends and making social connections with those on a similar wavelength. Improved circumstances and being able to find some harmony in daily living.

Reversed meaning

There are obstacles and difficulties which need to be addressed as they are getting in the way of true happiness. Self confidence and self esteem may not be at their best. It heralds a time of seeking out those who are trustworthy for a little emotional support. There is no need to be afraid of life. Opportunities are being missed because of the reticence to get involved and embrace life in all of its glory. Joy and hope are within reach if only you would look within and be kind to yourself instead of seeing all the negative qualities. Focus on the positives for a while and see the difference it has upon your circumstances.

Moon

Menstrual cycles and moods. Dreams, fantasies and illusions. Darkness and shadowy perceptions. The things that lurk in the shadows, lunacy and odd behaviour that may or may not be the result of hormonal imbalances (for females) arising as subconscious or repressed emotions and especially during the time of the full moon. Being overwhelmed by emotions with a lack of self control. Lonely path that must be walked in order to become aware of ones shadows. Walking into the unknown. There may be a tendency to see the worst in every situation until the positives are pointed out. Nightmares and vivid dreams, depression and anxiety related disorders. Feelings of being disconnected from friends and within close personal relationships. Sterility and coldness, or sexual inhibitions that have their root in the mind. Isolation. Fears. Phobias.

Reversed meaning
The situation described above has gone on for a long time and the person needs a lot of support and help for them to get better. Long term depression, isolation and illness. Advice should be sought from a professional and perhaps consider some form of therapy, healing or counselling as a way to move forward.

Sun

Psychic wholeness and integration of personality. Lightness of being. Lasting happiness. Fulfilment. Energy and vitality for life. Bright spark, being creative and innovative ideas are pouring out. Successful conclusion of activities and projects. Working well with others. Divine inspiration. Confident characteristics. Joy and contentment within partnerships and with friends and family. Getting the best out of life. Healthy relationships and communications. A state of being settled into one's life and radiating from within, bringing love, peace and joy to others.

Reversed meaning
Idealization may be an issue within relationships and not being content with the current partner. Dissatisfaction with one's circumstances, life and relationships in general. Preferring to fantasize rather then have actual meaningful contact. Perhaps there needs to be subtle changes to ones innermost desires and bring them into alignment with reality instead of imaginary perceptions. Perceived blockages and stagnation of personality.

Judgement

Waking up to one's destiny or calling in life. Seeing things from a different perspective with clarity and inspiration. Working towards a better future for all humanity. Considering others before oneself and altering priorities. Humanitarian pursuits. Helping, coaching and, or teaching others how to better themselves. Finding meaning and purpose in life and attracting others of a like mind, co-operating and collaborating on projects. Successful conclusion to projects. Completion, endings of long cycles and beginning new things.

Reversed meaning
Blockages caused by lack of self es- teem and inability to relate to others socially. Dislike of certain people or their ways of being. Intolerance. Having the sense of knowing that one has a higher purpose but not quite being able to reach it at this time. Never learning life's hard lessons and repeating mistakes. Not being able

to think outside of purely physical and material concerns. Not allowing oneself the time or space to be able to hear inner guidance and wisdom above the noise of thoughts and feelings and the thoughts and opinions of others. Cut off from intuition and inner knowing.

World Serpent/Universe

Grounded and centred in one's life. Fully integrated and open to experience all the joys and sorrows equally. Bringing dreams into manifestation. Access to inner wisdom and clarity. Knowing one's place in the world and where to put energies and attention. Freedom from distractions and attachments. Head and heart working in union. Stability, balance and growth at a steady rate. Places in Nature where we can re-connect and create sanctuary spaces to retreat to. Feelings of emotional calm and well-being. Creating a better life for oneself and doing the inner work of spiritual alchemy. Ceremonies, Initiations and rites of passage. Exceptionally skilled individuals. Knowing ones own strengths and weaknesses.

Reversed meaning

Out of touch with one's soul. Unforeseen circumstances and possibly ill health create difficulties that make growth and change impossible at this time. Feeling like giving up on hopes and dreams. Viewing others and self in a negative light. Taking on projects that are out of ones reach.

Missing important and crucial information. Unsettled way of life. Lacking direction. Feelings of loss and grief. Repressive and regressive tendencies. Abandoning plans without thought for consequences. Crisis.

Understanding the suits of the Minor Arcana

The four suits of the Minor Arcana parallel the four suits found in traditional playing card decks of Clubs, Hearts, Spades and Diamonds.

They are represented in traditional Tarot decks as Wands, Cups, Swords and Pentacles.

Each suit represents a world that contains certain types of experiences and also corresponds to a part of the cycle of the year, with each suit representing a season. The Minor Arcana can be understood as representing the worlds of spirit, thought, emotion and sensation. This suit represent the influence of spirit and the spiritual world upon us and anything can come to us from this place arriving in the form of divine or inspired actions, thought, deeds and, or, spiritual messages received from guides or helpers that come to us in times of need.

- Wands – Spirit
- Swords – Thoughts
- Cups – Emotions
- Pentacles – Sensations

Wands – clubs – batons - staffs

This suit represent the influence of spirit and the spiritual world upon us and anything can come to us from this place arriving in the form of divine or inspired actions, thought, deeds and, or, spiritual messages received from guides or helpers that come to us in times of need.

Once the light of the spiritual flame has been kindled within then it burns with an intense fire, with heat and passion as we feed it with the fuel of our intellect as we learn and explore in the spiritual realms.

Hearts / Cups / Chalices

We can think of this realm or world of emotions, whether these are good or bad, as the strong feelings for anything that we experience or have experienced in life. Everything that makes us who we are. Our wishes, desires, projections and aspirations, all of which we carry on into the world of dreams every night when we go to sleep. Sometimes we can find answers and guidance during the dreaming process, and other times we are led by our emotions into certain actions. Emotions can be roused by thoughts, music, interactions with others, past experiences or even outcomes that are wished or longed for!

Spades / Swords / Storm

This is the place of intellect, thought and rational intelligence or the realm of the Mind. This is where we spend a lot of our waking life thinking, analysing, and in critical observation of everything that we experience.

What we think about determines the kind of experiences that we draw towards us so if you are a person inclined towards worry and negative destructive patterns, this may be the hardest part of the learning journey to conquer those thought processes and change them to alter the mental world in which you live, so that you can stop attracting negative things, situations and people. Transforming the way that you think can change your world completely and the more open you are to new thoughts, ideas and ways of perceiving the more chance you have of creating positive, lasting change.

Pentacles / Discs / Diamonds

Pentacles represents the physical world and everything that comes with materiality ie, finance matters, security, growth or lack of wealth, possessions, work, home life, social and domestic environments, relationships with friends and loved ones and so on. Also you need to consider here the land upon which you live and your at- titude towards it, and respect for Nature and the natural world. Especially the importance of conservation of woodlands and green spaces. Developing a personal relationship with sacred places or power places in nature can become an important part of the spiritual development process. These can be discovered if you intentionally journey and meditate outside in nature. This is especially important for young children so important to maintain thir connection with nature, and teach them about the cycles of life, progression, nurturing, birth, and death.

Nature has so much to teach us all and it is imperative to keep that close connection with the earth so as not to lose your way. In each suit of the Minor Arcana the cards are numbered 1 to 10 and each suit also has four Court Cards associated with it. In some decks these suits have slightly different names.

You could use a set of normal playing cards to read with using the following interpretations, or as part of a read- ing which uses the Major and Minor Arcana of the Tarot together. Until you get to know the cards well you can practice reading with just the Major Arcana and the three card method, or just the Court Cards.

Experiment and see what works for you.

Wands – Clubs – Fire
Swords – Spades - Air
Cups – Hearts – Water
Pentacles – Diamonds – Earth

Think of the Aces as the source of each of the Suits. Each ace is the outflowing of that particular element into the sphere of sensation of the practitioner. When working with the Archetypes of the major Arcana the four Aces are the opening influence. To begin with you could get acquainted with the elements over the course of a year using each ace as a focal point, or meditation subject for becoming more attuned to the seasonal cycles.

The symbols of the treasures themselves hold within them a key to understanding, acquiring/making magical weapons that are associated with each of the Elements.

Wand – trained mind of Initiate.
Sword – the intellect used as a tool.
Cup – emotions and the astral plane.
Pentacle – four elements and spirit functioning as a whole.

For example the Spring Equinox brings with it great change and the tides that move at that time of the year can cause all kinds of trouble for the student. With the howling winds and unsettled weather as we begin to come out of hibernation in the northern hemisphere and into the rebirth of Spring, the mind begins to awaken from its slumber.

Spring Equinox – Summer Solstice Sword
Summer Solstice – Autumn Equinox Cup
Autumn Equinox – Winter Solstice Pentacle

Winter Solstice – Spring Equinox Wand

Aligning with the cycle of progression through the elements changes at each of the points where the sun stands still, and at the balance points of light and dark.

Use these as focal points to connecting with the source or ace of each element allows you to spend time with each element during the seasons. Try putting the corresponding ace out on your altar at the times above.

Minor Arcana / Pip Card Interpretations

Wands / Clubs – Spiritual Influence

1. Wands

Source of Inspiration. Taking the lead in ones life. Creative energy of the will. Leaving the past behind. Banishing external negative influences. Being reliant on ones own spiritual values. Self Mastery and strength from within. Physical and emotional and spiritual working together in union. Having the courage of ones own convictions. Brand new ideas and visions formulating.

Reversed: Lack of enthusiasm and external influences are corrupting thought processes. Disappointment in relationships. Dissatisfaction with life. Outlook is dull and mundane. Lack of insight.

2. Wands

State of serenity after rites of passage or an initiation. Creativity in abundance. Looking ahead and planning for the future. Self created pioneers and those that move beyond thought into action. Picking a path or a tradition. Bold actions and motivation. Affirmations and desires coming to fruition. Moving into new disciplines. Resolute in actions and staying firm in ones beliefs.

Reversed: Disagreements, ungracious and undignified behaviour. Plans going awry due to lack of thought and planning. Bad decisions. Impatience. Lack of discernment and observation.

Considering ending a long term friendship or partnership. Loss of a close personal relationship. False friends. Cowardice.

3 Wands.

Springtime. Putting down roots or laying foundations for the future. Realisation of ones dreams and beginning the journey towards success. Bringing in and maintaining equilibrium. Positive connections and contacts. Achieving greatness, fame and notoriety. Independence and achievements. Looking at all of the details and fine print before making any decisions. Knowing who we are and where our place is in life. Getting rid of com- plications and using all of ones skills wisely. Cooperation and hard work.

Reversed: Skewed perspective. Attitude of distrust towards others. Stuck in a rut. Perceiving ambition as arrogance. Bad or unsolicited advice. Thwarted ambition and stifled behaviour. Incompatible relationships. Stagnant thinking. Endings. Neglect.

Not getting the help that is needed for positive change.

4 Wands.

Working well in partnership with others. Stability and ability to work under stressful or difficult conditions. Minds that think alike. Logic, reason, and spontaneity. Projects coming to a successful conclusion. Success after careful and deliberate planning. Harmony, happiness, health and well-being. Listening to inner guidance and settling into a peaceful way of life. Getting recognition for talents and work.

Reversed: Getting into power struggles and personality conflicts. Distracted and subdued by the opinions of obstructive people. Environment is not conductive to progression. Insincerity and thinking or acting without care for the consequences. Harsh words, anxiety and criticism of self and others. Distance from negative situations and people is required before there can be any peace of mind.

5 Wands

Disturbances, strife and mania need to be overcome. Being strong and steadfast. Complex situations involving conflict and mind games. Hard work and competition. Sticking up for your self and making decisions based on what is best for you right now. Making some tough choices in life. Change for the better.

Reversed: Encounters with dishonest people and situations. Perspective required and looking at the larger picture. Stand back and take stock. Avoidance of conflict. Put things into order of importance to lessen burdens. Knowing who to trust and who to stay away from to avoid confrontational situations. Being aware of charlatans. Clearing out and using all of ones resources.

6 Wands

Past projects and work that is beginning to get recognition. Hearing the call to a vocation. New ventures on roads that have never been travelled before. Public personas and attention in the media. Lots of communication. Teaching others how to achieve and lead. Realization of direction, dreams and ambitions. Set to achieve greatness. Completion of something which leads the way to beginning something anew.

Reversed: Lack of faith in ones own abilities and gifts. Letting others lead the way. Shy and awkward behaviour. Unable to commit to anything, lack of self esteem and motivation for anything in life. Steering away from contact with others. Delays, worry and anxiety. Unwise choices. Damaged reputation because of lies and untruths being spread by others.

7 Wands

Influences from the other- worldly realms. Non conformist attitudes. Being unique. Emergence of skills. Walking a solitary path. Putting all of ones effort, attention and will into new ventures. Hard work will pay off. Unwavering confidence in ones abilities in chosen direction. Becoming the star you were always meant to be. Meeting challenges head on. Mystical experiences and listening to inner voice in the face of unsolicited criticism an opinion from other people. Grace. Dexterity. Freedom of choice.

Reversed: Feelings hurt. Dejection, worry, and fear of failing. Avoiding hard work and not taking responsibility for ones own actions. Lessons learned and must now move on, let go and release the past. Coming to the end of a difficult period. Unburdened and feeling lighter after a release. Hard knocks to confidence and self esteem. Road to recovery.

8 Wands.

No time to waste. The time is NOW. Sudden, directed and explosive bursts of creative energy. Need to keep things going until completion. Forward momentum. Speed and agility. Direction of will towards completion and successful conclusions. Motivation. Journeying. Burdens lifted. Pushing the envelope and cutting edge. Getting ahead in ones chosen field. Happiness and contentment after hard work and a job well done. Walking ones path to success.

Reversed: Getting carried along in the drama of others. Loss. Disagreements and harsh words in close personal relationships. Expect things to go awry unless behaviour can be changed. Wasteful attitudes and apathy towards those who are doing well. Hasty de- cisions and thoughtlessness. Causing trouble for others. Significant lack of personal development. Attempting to control others rather than look at own self.

9 Wands.

Initiations, rites of passage, graduating in terms of coming through difficulties and gaining wis- dom. Patience, diligence, and setting out on new ventures. Making wise choices using past life experiences as a reference point. Being adaptable and self reliant. Helping others make decisions. Long term planning and goal setting. Looking into the future. Temporary respite from difficulties Seeing things clearly with perspective. Using inner resources and confidence to jump hurdles and obstacles.

Reversed: Not being able to see or appreciate the needs of those around you. Stifled imagination and standstill creatively. Being too open with ideas and sharing with the wrong people. Having trouble relating and finding things difficult. Feeling disconnected from everything. Confusion and misdirection. Reacting from past situations rather than what is actually happening. No commitment or will power. Disinterest. Hard work for little reward. Centred around self with no thought or consideration for anything else.

10 Wands.

Delegation required due to being overburdened after having taken on too much. Previous situations have become unbearable and somehow must be diffused. Finding time for ones self in amongst the burdens of mundane things. Making space. Difficulties within close personal relationships require new solutions and thinking outside the box. Inner strength must be sought. Releasing attachments to people, things and situations. Sharing and asking for help to relieve some of the pressure. Awareness of false friends and slander. Prioritising and letting go of things which are not within reach.

Reversed: Being aware that there are difficult times ahead, Readying ones self for drama and knowing when and when not to get involved. Freedom from bonds and seeing light at the end of the tunnel. Looking for ways through adversity. Feelings of mistrust and doubt. Feeling like things are spiralling downwards. Giving out ill considered advice to others. Refrain from speculation. Taking one day at a time. Recognising power struggles and finding ways to resolve them without conflict. Learn- ing patience and tolerance of others misgivings.

Suit of Swords / Spades - Thoughts

1 Sword

Unlimited potential and release of negative thinking processes. Realisation of ones creativity and limitless force that comes from within. Cutting through the mire of confusion and seeing things with absolute clarity. Acting with integrity, using Create new beginnings for ones self. Cutting ties with the past. Accuracy and sensible decisions, judging things with all of the facts to hand. Foresight and the ability to see the error of previous modes of thinking. Changing outdated beliefs. Healthy thinking processes. Revelations and illuminating untruths. Order restored and precision of thought. Honesty and forthright behaviour towards self and others.

Reversed: Feelings of detachment and clouded judgement, lack of common sense and mental instability. In extreme cases paranoia and unwarranted distrust. Cold and unemotional people. Corruption and immoral behaviour. Depression, destructive thoughts, deceit, suspicion and mistrust. A time of making the wrong choices. Realisation of negative thinking patterns and correction of behaviour required before progression can be made. Rash decisions need to be avoided. Best to wait until thinking clearly to avoid misfortune.

2 Swords

Sovereignty. Being patient and using correct application of skills. Rest, respite and headspace. Balance and equilibrium re- stored after difficulties. Investigative period, analysis, and constructive self reflection. Working well within a partnership. Diplomatic attitude. Neutrality. Free and easy communication on all levels. Considering all possibilities and making rational and logical choices, without emotions clouding judgement. Temporary respite. Acting with fair- ness towards all those seeking attention and help. Receipt of good advice. Reading, studying, taking in lots of information. Having the advantage of being able to be objective in situations where others struggle to see the bigger picture. Peace and solitude.

Reversed: Disturbances in thinking. Contradictions and conflicting advice received. Distance required in close personal relationships. Temporary separations. Strife, torment, mental anguish during disagreements. Conflict from differences in opinion. Struggling to come to terms with opposing beliefs. Seeking solutions to resolve differ- ences rather that staying in the conflict zone. Space, thinking time and peaceful environment required to re- gain balance. Recognising dishonesty in self and others, and destructive behaviour patterns that require re-adjustment.

Personal development needed.

3 Swords

Putting on a brave face in adverse situations. Unstable frame of mind due to loss and grief. Much sadness and difficult situations that require great courage to face the darkness. Feelings of being overwhelmed. Too many thoughts. Despair and hard life lessons. Imbalance and karmic issues. Sorrow, grief and suffering can teach great lessons. Afterwards there is a greater capacity for joy. Working through inner torment. Healing a broken heart. Resisting change. Times of hardship when you must learn to look inward and draw upon inner strength.

Reversed: Unhealthy, destructive and constricting relationships that foretell a miserable outlook. Shallow and toxic individuals. Painful experiences and separation. Love based on what the other can do for you, or you can do for them, rather than what you can both bring to each other. Standstill and being unable to see what to do to resolve potentially explosive situations. Retreating inward. Defeat. Something needs to change. Guilt and lack of insight.

4 Swords

Finding peace in solitude. Period of withdrawal from stress and anxiety. Clarity and vision after a time of turmoil and distress. Taking a step back and reflecting in ones safe environment. Working well on ones own. Independent action and thought. Making decisions and acting on ones own initiative. Brief pause for thought and reflection after great difficulties. Reflecting upon recent events and gaining clarity. Re- treat into safe space for introspection. Rest, relaxation and contemplation. Listening to ones own inner wisdom and guidance before action of any kind. Inner work, meditation and retreating from worldly concerns.

Reversed: Feelings of isolation and disconnectedness within close per- sonal relationships. Disappointment and lack of clarity. Lack of personal space and privacy and making wild assumptions about people, things and situations that have no bearing on reality. Having no direction or purpose and being easily led astray. Persons who enjoy making trouble for others. Unsolicited or wrong guidance given. Thoughts are disjointed and and scattered, no clarity or insight.

5 Swords

Discontent and strife within close personal relationships. Fabricating untruths to distract from ones own failings and faults. Grief, worry, Loss. Thinking too much of ones self and being given humbling situations. Losing stability or having power taken by others. Dealing with sneaky individuals whose moral compass points to causing trouble and conflict for others. Overbearing behaviour within relationships and trying to control everything in ones environment. Not being able to accept truth. Lying to ones self. Getting involved in petty gossip and bad mouthing others. Deliberately planning to cause grief for another. Inability to let go of the past and things that have happened. Holding on to negative thoughts and patterns.

Reversed: Temporary respite from stressful situations and conflict. Taking care to avoid confrontations. Recognising loss of self confidence and working towards feeling better about ones self. Building self esteem. Disappointing revelations. A time of resolving problems and keeping out of the way when situations with others are brewing that are not of your concern.

Feelings of being overwhelmed mentally which causes anxiety. Changing perspectives and starting to see things a little more clearly. Recovering from loss or trauma at the hands of another. Knowing when to withdraw from potentially explosive situations.

6 Swords

Being able to effectively communicate with others after a period of withdrawal. Processing past situations and being able to move forward after difficult circumstances. Open and receptive to movement in life. Meeting new people and making contacts. Things getting better after a time of stress and burdens. Technology and communication. Putting ones self in a better environment which allows time and space to reflect, work and expand. Change after revelations. Understanding ones path and embracing communication on all levels. Seeing with clarity of perception. Bright future ahead. Latent talents and abilities are being recognised. Working with others as well as working on ones own for the greater good. Higher vision and pioneering mindset. Physical or mental move in to a better space.

Reversed: Thoughts are drowning in emotions. Going it alone on a path which ostensibly cuts off lines of help and communication with those who could have been of assistance. Making bad decisions and choices without having enough information. Walling oneself in and building barriers. Anger issues. Looking for fast solutions which may not be ideal rather than looking at the long term and ramifications of those outcomes. Failing to do the right thing. Things not working out as one had hoped. Not being given the whole truth.

7 Swords

Mind centred and thoughts are dominant over the heart and intuitive functions. Erratic and unconventional behaviour. One of a kind personalities. Sometimes indicates those who are inclined towards manipulation of others for purely selfish means. Taking precautionary measures to ensure one is not taken for a ride by someone pretending to be something they are not. Being aware of vulnerabilities and never allowing oneself to be taken for a ride. Considering splitting from current husband/wife/partner. Conspiring and conjecture. An unconventional attitude may need to be taken to solve problems and difficult situations. Struggling with hearing ones own thoughts amid the chaos. Use of visionary frame of mind that can allow for detachment from actual situations to assist in coming to terms with problematic people.

Reversed: Taking things literally and making a big deal of little things thereby missing out on great opportunities. Being shy and restricting ones self as a consequence. Giving too much away about ones personal life and finding it difficult to know who to trust. Impatience and mistrust. Being careless in thought and deed. Being compelled into action instead of making informed choices. Removal of stagnant energy and blockages which have restricted clear thinking. Taking alternative approaches and cultivating different ways of doing things that are situation specific. One way does not fit all. Be creative in approaches to dealing with difficulties. Non committal. Having patience and waiting to see how things pan out instead of trying to be in control.

8 Swords

Removal of the persona or created personality that no longer portrays ones values or actual stand- point in life. Taking responsibility for ones actions and part in creating any problems that may have surfaced. Frightened to be oneself for fear of being judged by others. Falling into the negativity trap. Difficulty in trusting others or reaching out to make new contacts. Finding communication difficult. Running on impulses and instincts and feeling imprisoned or trapped in circumstances that are a direct result of ones own choices. Attachments and obsessions that require release. Irrational feelings of guilt or anxiety, worry and stress when things are not as bad as they could be. Struggling in social situations. A period of illness that may take time to recover from and require assistance of close friends, family and self healing before normality can be resumed.

Reversed: Getting to the bottom of where difficulties arise. Recognising negative thinking and re-programming the mind for a healthier out- look. Sensing limits and boundaries that have been largely self created and working towards release. Oppressive attitudes released which in turn brings about a much better environment in which to live, work and play. Clarity of perception and honing ones mental skills, bringing things into focus after a period of confusion and disorientation which will then allow expansion of awareness. Recognising and dealing with addictive behaviour. Getting help from outside agencies such as counsellors or healers to release negative and obsessive thought patterns. Getting to the stage where there is an inner knowing of what has to happen to move forward and regain balance. Acceptance of circumstances.

9 Swords

Suffering shock at recent revelations that were not previously known. Spiritual awakenings and an increase of sensitivity. Misplaced loyalties and self critical attitude undermine confidence. Heightened awareness. Fears and anxiety getting out of control. A period of feeling low or deflated, after effects of cruelty. Actions of others has a detrimental effect on the health and well-being of the seeker. Having to face hard situations and fight off feelings of despair and lack of self worth.

Too many thoughts and intrusions by others. Lack of peace. Learning hard life lessons. In extreme cases there may be suicidal thoughts or thought of harm to self. Nightmares and un-balanced lifestyles.

Reversed: Discovery of behaviour that has been ongoing which could be termed abusive. Recognising destructive cycles and patterns and choosing to break them. Aftermath of a breakdown in communication within a close personal relationship and maybe even a temporary separation or breakup of a relationship. Focus on positive aspects and break destructive and negative modes of thinking. Learn from mistakes. Not repeating the same situations over and over again. Finding it difficult to act with integrity and with moral values. Feelings of or actual isolation. Beginning to come to the end of a period of discontent and getting help to let go of self limiting belief structures. Challenging behaviour.

10 Swords

Betrayal by those who were formerly perceived to be acting with the seekers best interests. A breaking down of something to make way for a fresh perspective and new understanding. Resolution of difficulties. True motives are brought out into the light. Judging others or being judged oneself. A time of unfortunate circumstances, sorrow and sadness which may bring about terminations in friendships or current ways of being. Too much focus on the pursuit of material wealth leaves no room for experience in other areas of life. Coming out of situations that have built a stronger personality with more faith in one's own abilities. Taking time to reflect and be grateful for what you have and realise that nothing ever stays the same, and the only thing that you can be sure of is that there will always be change.

Reversed: Something has thwarted progression, and to move on now it is time to let go of outmoded ideals and issues and feel a great weight being lifted. A sense of relief and feeling better in oneself after having avoided a potentially risky or dangerous situation. Gaining clarity, wisdom and under- standing through life experience and learning to be able to forgive others who have acted in a less than desirable manner. Now is not the right time for decision making as judgements may be clouded and until those clouds have cleared err on the side of caution.

Suit Cups/Hearts – Emotions

1 Cup

Outpouring and receipt of Love in all of its forms. Can signify marriage, conception, births and unions. Spiritual experiences and those of an Artistic nature. Feelings of warmth, caring and love. Beauty, fulfilment, inspiration and joy. The womb of the mother and the act of nurturing. The vessel into which we receive and give Love. The Grail. Healing. Art. Music. Negativity over- come. New ventures.

Visions and psychic experiences. Spirituality. Releasing buried emotions. Creativity in abundance. Success. Selflessness. Possible Marriage proposal. Security. Vitality. Easily led. Honesty.

Reversed: Sadness and loss of Love. Depression, emptiness and disinterest. Erecting barriers and boundaries. Despair. Darkness. Distrust. Separation. Immaturity. Emotional disfunction. Denial. Unhappiness in relationships. Succumbing to inhibitions. Fear of close contact. Tears and feelings of loneliness within close personal relationships.

2 Cups

Merging of two souls. Unity. Differences reconciled. Bonding and sharing experiences. Romance. Dreaminess. Love at first sight. Sensitivity to others. Harmony. Compassion. Imagination. Immaturity. Clinging. Devotion. Compatible relationships and harmonious situations. Forgiving those who have wronged us.

Tolerance and resolution of conflict. Sympathetic and compassionate people. Two functioning in harmony as one.

Reversed: Arguements and disruptive behaviour. Relationship difficulties. Contempt. Lack of trust and pessimistic attitudes. Deception uncovered. Regret and loss of desire. Apathy. Coldness and indifference. Loneliness and confusion. Emotional issues. Endings and temporary separations. Misunderstandings and broken promises. Inexperience in Love. Envy. Difficult relationships. Caution advised. Bad choice in partner. Differences outweigh positives. Unfulfilled desires and lack of concern for the needs of others.

3 Cups

Declarations of love and commitment. Engagements. Trust. Security and family responsibilities. Pay attention to omens and signs. Emotional needs being met. Pregnancy and birthing of projects. Flow of energy and love. Coming to new levels of understanding and co- operation within established relationships. Child birth and child rearing. Social gatherings and celebrations. Mutual respect and understanding in relationships. Flow of energy without restriction. Harmonious partnerships and relationships.

Reversed: Suffering and disappointment in love. Pessimism and unhappiness. Situations arise which test strength of individual and partnerships. Receipt of bad news. A need to look at ones behaviour and resulting consequences. Crisis and drama. Attachments and obsessions. Greed and hostility. Grasping. Open display of bad feeling toward others. Lack of empathy. Changes are necessary before progress can be made. Exploitation. Sexual gratification with no real feeling.

4 Cups

Strong, healthy and positive relationships. Idealism. Fond of reflection. Temporary pause for introspection. Boredom perhaps. Solitude and respite. Hesitation to act. Apathy and tiredness. Certain amount of contentedness but with a sense of discomfort, working through underlying issues before happiness. Relaxation. Emotions in a state of temporary rest. Feed and nourish the soul. Pessimism and tendency toward negativity must be overcome. Individual coming to a better understanding of themselves spiritually. Growth. Security and stability though feeling stuck in some way. New interests and widening horizons may be a way forward.

Reversed: Unable to see clearly. Sexual problems as a result of mental anxiety. Self obsession. Animosity towards friends and family. Temporary period of stasis and staleness. Brooding and malaise. Exhaustion. Passive aggressive state of being. Unwilling to be open and honest. Feelings of self pity. Depression and inertia. Inability to overcome personal issues. Blame. Avoidance of responsibility.

5 Cups

Sorrow, loss and dejection. Ending of a relationship or a separation. Wasted energy and resources. Difficulties within close personal relationships. Failed romance or Marriage. Sorrow, disappointment in Love. Rejection. Deception. Lack of communication. Looking for the light at the end of the tunnel. Bringing about new situations and beginning the healing process. Emotional disfunction. Overreacting and not seeing things as they truly are. Look for positives and refocus. Avoid brooding on what may have been. Everything for a reason though it may not be apparent at the time. Decline of a relationship and love lost in a previously happy union. Marriage troubles. Frustration.

Reversed: Prolonged suffering and grief. Sadness and loneliness. Severe emotional pain and grief at the loss of something or someone close. A bereavement whether at the loss of a relationship or a person. Life changing trauma. Ending of a happy situation. Distancing oneself from others. Coping mechanisms. Attempts to avoid pain. Emotionless. Shallow people. Perhaps being taken for granted by others. Coldness. Indifference. Time required to heal from emotional wounds. Sometimes can signify a long period of sorrow coming to an end.

6 Cups

Creativity in abundance. Sincerity. Memories. Sharing and good feelings. The early stages within romance. Developments. Gaining emotional strength. Sincerity and honesty. Beginnings of a pleasant time. Compatibility between partners. Strong emotional ties to others past and present.

Kindness shown to others in the past comes full circle and we are shown kindness by others. Ready for anything. New friends and relationships. Contact with Elemental energies. Appreciating the simple things in life. Reappearance of old friends stirring up emotions and pleasant memories.

Reversed: Past situations which are still having an unpleasant effect on present life. Tendency to live in the past. Secret relationships and longing for times that are perceived as being better than the current situation. Sometimes can signify rekindled flames, or past lovers interfering or causing disturbances in present situation. Recurring dreams which one must pay attention to and decode. Insensitivity to others. Cooling desires perhaps. Mistrust. Incompatibility being highlighted. Envy. Parting of the ways.

7 Cups

Uncharted territory. Rising emotions and indecisions. Unique and eccentric individuals. Prone to fantasy. Unexplained occurrences and psychic episodes. Visions. Self deception. Unable to control emotions. Having difficulty making decisions. Intense experiences. Creative imagination. Finding it difficult to concentrate on one thing. Neglecting important things. Compulsive behaviour. Addictions and clouded judgements. Waste. Not taking advantage of opportunities when they present themselves.

Reversed: Regaining ones senses. Coming out of a period of confusion. Making changes to habits and recognising when fantasy is allowed to take place of actual events. Having standards that require to be maintained with integrity. Foresight or prophetic dreams. Attaining greater understanding in situations that have previously been misunderstood. Wishful thinking. Gifts being offered that appear too good to be true. Reality check. Getting facts straight before making any decisions. Practicality instead of day-dreaming. Careful consideration. Unsure how to approach taboo subjects within relationships.

8 Cups

Avoidance of truth. No appreciation of others and what they do. Taking the safe road which in turn means no progression. Considering making changes. Unsatisfied with life and relationships. More interested in appearance. No depth. Missed opportunities.

Fizzling out of relationships. Possible new starts. Feeling unsettled and restless. Always seeking and never finding. Suffering delusions. Chasing after the impossible. Preferring to make assumptions rather than find out truth. Important matters are being ignored that need attention. Irrational state of mind. Leaving the past behind and seeking new ventures and could mean a change in residence or employment. Unreliability. Incompatibility and changing needs mean that a relationship cannot go on the way it has been. Separation may be the best way until final decisions can be made.

Reversed: When this card appears reversed it may indicate the ending of a situation or a relationship is not the right thing to do at this time. Taking a less defensive attitude per- haps, caution and careful consideration before making and choices that will seriously affect the future in a negative way. Dealing with inhibitions and moving out of negative attitudes. Making improvements and building bridges in relationships. Taking time to appreciate the good things in life. Gratitude, respect and being open. Becoming more aware of everything.

9 Cups

Favourable outlook. Optimism. Creative outlets. Painting, Art, Music. Performances. Having the courage of ones convictions. Realization of desires and wishes being fulfilled. Positive and trusting relationships. Loyalty. Ability to see through difficulties. Kindness. Gain. Composure. Equality in partnerships. Faith. Sustainability. Love and friendships. Enjoyment from helping others. Free from distractions and worries. Contentment. Mutual affection in relationships. Caring and considerate in sexual relations.

Reversed. Fallow period. Foolishness and con- ceit. Superficial. Losing faith. Blockages and emotional turmoil. Consequences of making bad decisions. Complacency. Apprehension. Blind faith. Imagined security. Thinking much of ones self.

Absence of depth in close personal relationships. Unable to see things from any other perspective than ones own. Misunderstandings and lack of empathy. Not taking the feelings of others onto consideration. Maybe the wrong choice in partner. Too much concern for outward appearances.

10 Cups

Mastery. Success. Joy. Achievements. Inspirations. Over- sensitivity. Conclusions. Growth and happiness. Family. Community. Stable environments and groups of people working together for the same cause. Sometimes there may be underlying concerns that have not been brought to the surface yet. Psychic disturbances. Overall a happy marriage or partnership is signified. Satiation.

Reversed: Personality clashes or one person disrupting an otherwise idyllic situation. Sibling rivalry perhaps or interference. Romantic or domestic problems. Jealousy causing issues. Emotional crisis, and/or, spiritual darkness. Secrets. Disappointment from unfulfilled desires, hopes and dreams. Affection that is not returned. Danger. Violation. Discord. Rejection. Animosity. Immoral behaviour.

Suit of Pentacles / Discs / Diamonds – Sensations

1 Pentacle

New beginnings and especially new ventures and business startups. Purchases. Promotions. Inner worth. Recognition for hard work. Spirituality over wealth must be realised. Safety. Investments. Security. Creativity flourishing. Strength. Physical realm and sensual pleasures. Practical matters. Family ties and good relationships. Animal lovers and nature enthusiasts. Status. Promotions. Skills. Fame. Enjoyment of sexuality. Physical needs being met.

Reversed: Bankruptcy. Fraud and deceit in business transactions. Negativity. Wrong or incorrect information. Wasting resources. Taking short cuts. Apathy. Bad investments. Obsessed with material wealth. Materialism over spirituality. Untrustworthy individuals. Stability upset. Crime. Guilt in relationships. Building walls. Possible physical illness. Over indulgence. Low standards.

2 Pentacles

Juggling lots of balls in the air simultaneously. Early stages of a business venture. Inner voice. Taking educated risks. Getting ones finances in order. Circumstances are improving after difficulties. Reliable friends and colleagues. Trust. Determination and ambition. Equilibrium and balance. Investing for the future. Practical advice.

Ambition and drive. Budgeting. Transitions. Being in the moment, fully present. Sensible and down to earth attitudes. Making small gains. Ventures that are worthwhile.

Reversed: Impulsive and ill considered deci-sions. Carelessness. Resisting change at all costs. Unable to go with the flow. Stress. Small minded attitudes. Indecisive and moody individuals. Lack of motivation or sustained interest. Inaction. Incapable. Trying to do things too fast. Attention to detail is required. Confusion. Turbulence in relationships. Angst. Lacking commitment. Immaturity. Frustration. Silly behaviour. Waste. No consideration for others. Nothing is permanent. Fluctuating.

3 Pentacles

Freelancing. Specialist knowledge. Teaching. Professional. Rewarding work. Material concerns. Marketing and promotion. Being immersed in ones work. Recognition of talents and skills. Art. Commissions. Hardworking. Creative people. Meeting deadlines. Approval. Contracts. Paid ones worth. Honesty in business dealings. Care and concern for close family and friends. Planning and laying foundations for the future.

Reversed: Giving up before completion. No appreciation for ones skills. Being taken for a ride. No morals. Using unfair methods to get ones own way. Thankless tasks. Harsh criticism. Putting on a show. Not revealing true feelings. Dislike of real talent. Commercialism killing originality. Plagiarism or being plagiarized by others. False attitudes. Not being true to ones self. Trying to impress others. Feeling under pressure to conform.

4 Pentacles

Influence and Gain. Work that is towards definite goals. Progression and momentum. Large scale projects. Taking things one step and a time. Slow and method- ical. Careful consideration. A little too much focus on the physical to the detriment of other things. Extremes. Avoid rigid regimes. Strong foundations upon which to work.

Taking stock of everything before planning next move. Stabilising. Risk of stagnation and blockages if things become stale. Temporary respite from troubles that shouldn't become a way of life. Don't create a prison for ones self.

Reversed: Unhealthy relationship with money. Finances in a mess. Crisis. Disorder and chaos. Caution is advised when making any deals. Getting out of a materialistic frame of mind. Loss of wealth and security. Ruin. Focus on the moment.

Suspicion and questioning the motives of others. Ill considered decisions that have far reaching consequences. Disempowerment. Less focus or con- cern for the future and take each day at a time. Dishonest transactions leading to trouble. Fear of risk taking and inhibitions. Clinging to things which should have been let go of voluntarily.

5 Pentacles

Power struggles, disagreements and arguments within close personal relationships. Depression. Change is needed. Financial difficulties casing ill health. Possible unemployment. Suffering and general feeling of being unwell. No productivity. Hardship. Waste. Lack of skills. Lifestyle change required. No one to turn to or too proud to ask for help. Self imposed limitations. Poverty and lack.

Lacking security and strength. Seeking help and support. Sharing burdens and lightening the load. Absence of love as a result of not being open to receive.

Reversed: Hopeless situation that is not helped by pessimistic attitude towards life. Negative thinking attracting more difficulties and problems as a result. Oppressive situations. Freedom and breaking out of routine. Insecurity. Disruptions in home life. Letting go. Making improvements to a domestic situation. Compromise. Stop worrying and prioritise in order of importance.

If it isn't top priority and is not needed any more then let go. Gaining new skills to help with better employment prospects.

6 Discs

Making good investments. Planning. Getting business or financial advice. Delegation. Hark work paying off. Hiring others to assist. Use intelligence for problem solving. Sharing good fortune with others. Energy exchanges, receipt of and giving of gifts. Paying debts or paying forward good karma. Being kind to others as a way of life. Generosity and benevolence. Moving out of debt. Effective management. Bonuses. Fair dealings. Gratitude. Love and equality within relation- ships. Giving and receiving of pleasure. Romance.

Reversed: Carelessness. loss of security, and or wealth. Feelings of being cheated or treated unfairly. Deception. Negativity. Untrustworthy characters need unveiled. Fraudulent motives. Getting involved with the community. Finding it difficult to secure decent employment. Mistreatment at the hands of others. Not seeing things clearly. Theft of property or being taken for granted.

7 Pentacles

Looking for work that is meaningful. Vocations. Unfulfilled lifestyle leads to behaviour problems. Feel- ing overburdened. Making foolish decisions. Natural talents have net been uncovered yet. Practicality and honing skills. Never give up. Perseverance, persistence and determination. Making use of what resources are available and not wasting time or energy on things that are unproductive and purely for monetary gain. Lack of faith in ones own abilities. Progress. Working towards a meaningful goal. Possible self employment or work that is of personal importance.

Reversed: Fulfilling duties and motivated by making money. Learning from mistakes that have been made in the past. Self doubt and inhibitions are being overcome. Material matters are improving significantly. Professional attitudes. Gaining strength and recovering from anxiety. Avoiding distractions. Lost opportunities. Unfinished projects and abandoned works. Getting stuck in a rut. Reticence to commit to anything. Lack of long term goals and objectives. Clearing out emotional blockages. Seeing things from a better perspective after rest and respite.

8 Pentacles

Getting ready for long term commitment of some kind. Confidence restored and gaining faith in ones self. Avoid distractions. New directions. Conclusion of a project. Job well done. Led by desire. Self employment, or apprenticeships. Moved out of poverty consciousness into abundance. Moral high ground. Careful attention. Lots of personal growth. Creative period begins. Going with instincts and morals. Secure future and working in harmony with others to achieve this. Deep commitment to another person or cause.

Reversed: No practicality. Work without rewards. Short term benefits outweighed by heavy responsibilities. A need for priorities. Lack of care and discipline. Maturity. Little gains for lots of effort. Work ethics leave a lot to be desired. Misunderstandings. Taking shortcuts in a n attempt to lighten the load. Too much focus on monetary gain. Fear of failure. No depth or commitment. Relationship at the present is not fulfilling needs and desired because there's no real emotional connection.

9 Pentacles

Talents being rewarded. Fame and notoriety. Wealth increasing. Higher purpose. Productivity beginning to slow down. Trust and security within relationships. Inheritances. Objectivity. Appreciation of nature. Relaxation and satisfaction of a job well done. Struggles have been overcome. Successful conclusion. Natural and healthy relationships. Mutual trust and respect. Being objective.

Position that has been worked hard for. Effort and sacrifices have been made to get to this stage. Enjoying all the pleasures and fulfilment of sexuality.

Reversed: Past misdeeds catching up. Guilt and anxiety over past behaviour. Corruption. Envy and jealousy. There is a need to act with integrity at all times. Superficiality. Mundane matters. No time or patience with others. Disturbances in thought patterns. Avoid temptation. Indecent behaviour. Difficulty handling finances. Resources have been used up. Greed.

10 Pentacles

Union. Completeness. Family support. Inheritances and windfalls. The bigger picture. Understanding and sensitivity to those close. Inner knowing and security, stability and calm that comes from within. Good advice being offered. Intelligent people. Great works. Satisfactory conclusions of large projects. Promotions. Gains. Wealth. Property and financial prowess. Family values, positive family influence and upbringing. Charming personalities. Help from friends and family. Material and emotional security. Unexpected wealth.

Reversed: Heavy burdens and family strife cause emotional disturbances. Drama and grudges being held. Stubborn attitudes causing conflict. Sibling rivalry and behavioural issues as a result of abuse. Sometimes can signify fighting over money after the loss of a loved one. Regret. One must recognise and resist negative influences whether they be from family or friends and step out on ones own. Emotional or sexual problems, inhibitions and anxiety as a result of upbringing.

Understanding Court personality cards

Apart from the major and minor arcana we also have the court cards which can be understood as being representative of certain personality types or physical, emotional, and stereotypical characteristics.

There are four court cards assigned to each suit, so there are four characters, two male and two female. Generally speaking there is a younger aspect and an older aspect of each pair of male/female characters associated with their respective suit, element, or world.

So for the suit of wands you have two older mature characters. King and Queen of wands. Then you have two younger male and female personalities as the Prince and Princess of Wands.

Esoterically they have significance as certain stages of transformation within the personality of the force they contain with reference to the particular world they have issued from. Eg, the burst of enlightenment received at the outset of a spiritual experience, which would be represented by the ace of wands, would become the physical manifestation of that experience into the earthly sphere of existence as the princess of wands. Or the formation of a thought at the level of the ace of swords, would come into manifestation in the physical world as the princess, in a concrete form, or thought that has been carried into manifestation as an idea or concept.

If you consider the pairing of the mature personalities as the king and queen, then the male and female characters of the prince and princess are younger versions of these same personalities. To know more about the function of Court Cards it would be prudent for the student to take them out of the deck and work just with those images on their own for a while. Attuning to the elements at the time of year signified on each image, and understanding each aspect in relation to the personality. It is possible to give a reading with those cards alone once you understand the significance of each of the central characters and their subjective meaning in relation to questions that have been asked.

NB: in relationship readings the court cards may represent individual characters who are known to the recipient of the reading. Sometimes they are are people with whom the querent may come into contact with at a later date. And in other situations they can be aspects of the enquirer that have yet to be explored.

If you or the person with whom you are reading do not recognise the characteristics of the person at the time of the reading, it may be that the court cards are suggesting latent aspects of the inquirers personality, or spiritual guides / ancestors that the enquirer is yet to encounter.

In other instances they can be read as representing a situation which has the characteristics associated with the court card. In some interpretations the court cards can also represent loved ones, relatives or friends who have passed over and it is something that you learn with experience of using the cards whether the person that is b ing referred to is still on the physical plane, and is possible having a subtle influence from another realm.

King of Wands / Clubs

Self reliant, family oriented, optimistic. Charming. Sociable and confident males. Approachable and friendly types. Inspiration to others. Efficient communicators. Kind natured and attractive in looks. Caring and loving, warm towards all. Walk their talk and are open and honest. Able to think on their feet. Goals within reach. Can be impulsive and thoughtless, sometimes unpredictable when younger. Fun to be around. Happy in their home environment. Live life with lots of enthusiasm. Change. New jobs or promotions. Travel. Open to opportunities and new ventures.

Negative traits: Abrupt and impatient. Tries to rush things and leaves many things unfinished. Jumping from fad to fad. Unable to see from the perspective of others, or outside of ones own environment. Not practical. Naive. Self centred and vain. Can indicate a change in sexual partners. Letting others lead instead of taking control of ones life. Afraid of failure. Fickle and changeable. Making hasty and ill thought out decisions.

Queen of Wands

Devoted wife and mother, skilful, confident, courageous and graceful. Confident hardworking professional women. Focussed and determined to succeed. Having courage and faith in one's own abilities. Supportive and passionate individuals. Strength, drive and positive attitudes.

Women who are adept at holding down a career or vocation and run a household. The gift of the present or staying in the moment. Kind, warm and loving female figures. Loyal and trustworthy. Lots of friendships. Grace and care for those close.

Negative traits: Clingy behaviour. Stubborn and irrational. Defensive nature without cause. Detached and unemotional. Shallow. Obsessed with own thoughts, self and ideas. Dogmatism. Unwillingness to accept any part of the blame or responsibility for ones actions. Overly concerned with material possessions or comforts.

Prince Wands

Visionary, entrepreneurial, multitalented, friendly male. Stepping out. Energy in abundance, self mastery. Self confident young males full of vitality and energy. Courageous and fearless. Perseverance and willpower to succeed. Creative blasts of energy. Authority figures. Competitive by nature. Inner Guide. Masculine energy. Overcoming difficulties and problems. Facing challenges head on with courage and integrity. Bringing out the best in ones character.

Negative traits: Ego inflation and self obsession. Neglecting family and home life. Work obsessed. Illusions and feelings of self importance that are not based in reality. Harsh criticism of others and avoidance of looking at ones own flaws. Putting out too much energy too quickly.

Princess of Wands

Wild young women, freedom, communicators, spontaneous behaviour, new skills. Seeker after new experiences. Sexually active. Carefree. Sense of adventure. Free spirit. Living in the moment and taking each day as it comes. Extreme behaviour. Alive. Enthusiastic. Embracing life. No inhibitions. Expressive and Sensual. Taking things to the extreme. Channeling abilities into worthwhile pursuits. Riding the waves of creativity. Deliberately setting out to achieve goals and dreams. Young female expressing and stepping out into their personality. New experiences and possibly first sexual encounters. Good news. Exciting times.

Negative traits: Refusal to move out of the past. Shallow and weak attitudes. Negative thinking. Thinking much of ones self when in reality people are unimpressed. Lacking in energy and social grace. Easily distracted and obstructive towards those who are progressing. Gossip. Unable to keep agreements. Broken promises.

King of Swords

Intelligent, quick minded individual. Innovative, technologically adept, sociable. Intelligent, quick minded and competitive older Males. Technologically adept. Can be distant, detached, cold and unemotional. Overactive imagination and prone to periods of hyperactivity and then withdraw into themselves. Scattered thoughts and never finishing projects once they have been started.

Overthinking, analytical and prone to negative thinking. Lots of ideas. Genius types. Egocentric. Effective communicators. Can be selfish. Avoidance of speculation and refocus may be required. Fresh perspectives. Struggling to see that taking a new direction or travelling new roads is essential. Attaining the truth of a matter. Uncovering deceit.

Negative traits. Spending too much time alone and becoming insular. Thinking too much. Overcomplicating things that could be simple. Getting involved in other peoples drama. Gossip and slander. Destructive or skewed logic.

Queen of Swords

Mature, sharp, witty, intelligent. Analysis and observation. Bright, cool, perceptive, collected and mature older women. Counsellors, tutors or teachers. Experts in their field of work. Rational and logical. Agile mind and attentive to detail. Problem solvers. Actors/Artists/Musical types. Organized individuals. Creating order out of chaos. Using natural skills and aptitudes. Greater perspective and seeing outside the box. Self reliant and honest. Avoidance of any thoughts of gaining advantage by manipulation of others. Getting a balanced perspective by analysis of all the good and bad points.

Negative traits: Cruelty and enjoyment of the distress of others. Self absorbed and views other people as a way of getting what they want. Seeking vulnerabilities to exploit. Domineering and controlling characters. Demanding and attention seeking. Manipulation. Faking. Shallow and devoid of real feeling or emotion.

Prince of Swords

Precise, critical, observer. Perfectionist, investigative nature. Reason. Improving mind. High minded and rational, sharp Males. Knowledge accumulation. Prone to sarcasm and with in difficult situations. Scientific and analytical. Natural intelligence. Complexity. Exploration of new ideas and fresh perspectives. Observant. Scientifically minded. Educated. Focussing will and clear thinking. Rational. Good at thinking outside the box. Investigative curious nature. Preference of logic over emotion. Try new things. Keep an open mind. Clear out the old to make way for new experiences. Truth coming to light. Patient application and study. Impatience with practical things when they don't go according to plan. Changing pace in life.

Negative traits: Lazy. Unable to get outside of ones own thoughts. Ignoring reality. Overly self critical. Demanding.

Obsessive and compulsive. Jealousy. Making ill informed choices due to preference of believing what goes on in the imagination rather than looking at actual facts. Grasping and needy, clinging to others out of desperate need. Playing mind games. Easily distracted. Cruelty.

Princess of Swords

Eccentric, complicated, original thinking, exploration, new and exciting things. Problem solving. Chaotic younger ladies. Trying to do too many things at once and living in a state of constant flux. Dislike of routine and order. Manic and wild thoughts. No focus or clarity. Distracted. Abstract thought and seeking, strange ideas and beliefs. Being ahead of the competition or way ahead of peers in terms of development. High functioning. Original. Unusual ideas and pastimes. Direct and open in dealings with others. New ideas and exploring new things. Something big is coming. Lots of messages. Confidence. Chang- es. Expression and communications. Taking a different approach in life.

Negative traits: Arrogant, manipulative. Disturbed. Out of balance. Behaving with no consideration for others. Paying too much attention to physical world to the detriment of inner worlds. Lack of social grace. Misguided and delusions of grandeur. Lies and manipulation of others for purely selfish motives.

King of Cups

Creative, deep, introspective men. Honest in dealings. Artistic – poetic type older male. Mysterious air. Visionary. Natural healer/shaman/empath. Emotionally warm and caring. High ideals. In touch with feminine side. A spiritual guide to others. One who regularly retreats to solitude for respite. Deep thinking. Initiations and rites of passage. Studying the behaviour of others. Spiritual development. Opening the heart. Retreating within.

Negative traits: Moody. Insecure. Pretending to care or have emotions. Misunderstood. Lack of morality. Attracting immoral and false people. No passion. Lack of dignity and mental health issues. Wrapped up in ones own world with no consideration for others. A need for healing. Creating difficulties for ones self. No conscience.

Queen of Cups

Intuitive, artistic women. dreamy and otherworldly. Ambition Motherly, caring women. Sensitives, Healers and counsellors. Family oriented. Children, hearth and home. Charming and sociable. Generous and supportive towards others. Good marriage or partnerships. Natural healing abilities and gifts of mediumship. Social and domestic pleasure.

Negative traits. Something has caused personality weakness or trauma that has had a long term effect. Hiding or retreating from close contact. Grudges. Easily manipulated by others and in turn reacts by controlling environment and others. Can be timid and indecisive. Overbearing with children rather than be- ing supportive. Can indicate underlying emotional issues that require therapy.

Prince of Cups

Poetic, artistic, News, messages, visionary ability, successful ventures. Introverted and shy young males. Dreaminess. Poets and visionaries. Solitary individuals. Nature loving. Caring. Deep.

Clairvoyant. Spiritually inclined. Inspired. intuitive Romantic and idealistic. Performance art. Natural ability to capture the imagination. One who understands the nature of sacrifice for the greater good. Musical and artistic abilities. Need to create. Natural healing abilities. Healing of self. Possible new romance on the horizon, or renewal of established relationship.

Negative traits. Self destructive. No vision or clarity of thought. Emotions cloud judgement. Giving too much away. Following instead of taking the lead and being manipulated by others. Apathy and illusory ideals. Short sighted vision of the future. Creative blockages. Inconsiderate of the needs of others.

Princess of Cups

Gifted, sensitive females. Delicate, romantic natured. Clairvoyance, creativity. Sensitive, highly imaginative young ladies. Fragile and empathic. Clairvoyant. Spiritual. Prone to drama and temperamental. Loving. Passionate. Innate ability to draw people and things towards them. Idealistic and high morality. Changeable and easily adapts to changing environments. Creativity in abundance. Soft and gentle. Charming and beautiful inside and out. Musical and or artistic.

Negative traits: Takes the words and actions of others to heart. Can be shy and retiring. Easily led. Projecting a personality that is not the true self but a mask of what she wants others to see. Self doubt. Stagnant or emotionless. Prone to fantasy rather than facing reality. Sentimental. Vanity and shallow pursuits. Inexperienced. Gullible.

King of pentacles / discs

Hardworking, strong, persistent men. Self reliant, nature loving, habitual, grounded. Practical matters. Practical, down to earth and very much connected to the land. Caretakers. Carpentry and skilled labour. Businessmen and grounded individuals who are not afraid of hard work. Wealth accumulated through labour. Wise. Sharp. Organised. Fearless. Warm, friendly and sociable. Domesticity. Home comforts and property management.

Negative traits: Constricted or stuck in old patterns of belief. Stubborn and single minded. Unable to empathise with the suffering of others. Selfish. Work obsessed. Has trouble showing emotions.

Queen of pentacles / discs

Mature, wise, friendly, productive women. Patience and diligence required. Strong willed females who are naturally adept at gardening and cultivation of plants and herbs. Land management and property development. Animal Lover. Strong willed. Nurturing. Caring. Altruistic. Big hearted. Warm loving personality. Selfless. Anchor for others. Happiest out in Nature. Generous.

Negative traits. Indecisive. Over thinking. Taking on too many of other peoples burdens as a way of distracting from personal problems. Health issues. Long term or chronic illnesses and restrictions or limitations. Unfulfilled potential. Prefers nostalgia than the present.

Prince of Pentacles. Farmers, builders, naturally talented men. Mastery, craftsmen-ship, reaping what one sows. Insight. Loyal, hardworking. Good with hands. Creative. Natural aptitude for bringing in money. Managing livestock. Prefers country living. Good natured. Handsome. In tune with the earth and all of its inhabitants. Moving slowly and deliberately. Painfully slow at making decisions. Even tempered and slow to excite, but once motivated there is no stopping them until the project has come to completion. Creating things with hands and tools. Practicality comes before anything else. Trustworthy.

Negative traits: Can be easily led. Distractions. Does not handle criticism well. Prone to building walls as a de- fence mechanism when feeling out of comfort zone. Prefers solitude. Can become unbalanced if out of contact with nature for too long. Natural affinity with the outdoors.

Princess of pentacles / discs

Naturally beautiful ladies. Reliant on instincts. Talking openly. Lots of changes. Warrior like strength. Shield maiden. Fiercely protecting those that she loves and cares for. In touch with Nature and the Earth Mother. Eco warrior type. In touch with feminine side and easily relates to man or beast. Equality. Fights for what is right. Rescues people as well as creatures to nurture and protect. Heroic.

Negative traits: Unapproachable. Aloof. Misunderstood. Solitude taken to the extreme. Stubborn and introverted. Struggles to see things clearly. Lack of objectivity. Too much concern for little things and missing opportunities in the process. Wasting time and resources. Not knowing when to quit. Obstinate.

This is not an exhaustive list of personalities depicted by the court cards but a starting point just to give you an idea of the different personality types. The negative traits mentioned are areas that may require work for the individual concerned whether that is you or the person for whom you are doing the reading.

It is my hope that this introduction to reading with the Initiates Way Tarot and the 22 Pathworkings allows you to begin your own journey into the Tarot, and the direction that it takes you is in your hands now. It is good practice to journal about your readings and your thoughts, feelings and experiences, dreams and insights that you have about each card as you get to know them.

Should you wish to work further with the Tarot I offer development groups and tuition using the pathworkings.

Email jade@esoteric-art.c.uk
www.esoteric-art.co.uk

Index

A
Abbot, Richard 191
Ace 31
Adiramled
 Divine Symbols 28
Afterlife 89
Alchemy 71, 108, 140, 147
Ancestors 248
Androgyny 141
Angel 64
Apocalypse 76
Aquarius 108
Arcadia 148
Archemides 26
Archetypes 12, 182
Arrogant 253
Artistic 253
Autumn 102

B
Birds 182
Bull 105

C
Carpentry 256
Celtic Church 60
Cernunnos 147
Cerridwen 146
Chakra 112
Chalices 214
Chaotic 253
Chariot 72, 76
Childbirth 37
Christ 147
Christianity 59
Conflict 152
Conqueror 79
Conversion 60
Court Cards
 Understanding 247–258
Crone 45
Crossroads 79

Crowley, Aleister
 Book of Thoth 140, 170
Cruelty 252
Cups 214, 233–258
Cycles 81

D
Dark Crystal 188
Dark Night of the Soul 131
De Gébelin, Count 161
De Lubicz. R.A. Schwaller 13
Death 126, 133, 178, 205
Demeter 42
Devil 142, 207
Diamonds 215
Dion Fortune 140
Discs 215
Divine Feminine 34
Dog Star 161
Dogmatism 249
Dreams 12, 30, 33, 162
Drowned Man 119, 123
Druidry 58, 62

E
Eagle 105
Earth 50
Ego 250
Egyptians 89
Elements 27
Emperor 199
Equinox 67, 81
Esoteric Art 9
Eternal life 126
Exoteric 9
Eye 125

F
Farmers 256
Fire 100
Fleur de lys 50

Fool
  Journey 11
  Path of the 125
Fortune 203

G
Gates of Dawn 178
Gemini 66, 173
Gender 10
Glastonbury 59
Gnostics 36
Golden Dawn spread 197
Gray, William G 7
Great Work 26
Greek Myth 126
Green Man 50
Guénon, René 1

H
Hag 45
Hanged Man 204
Happiness 113
Hecate 79
Hedwig 26
Heirophant 59, 200
Hermes 142
Hermit 90, 103, 202

I
Ibis 161
Infinity 88
Isis 37, 161

J
Jachin and Boaz 164, 186
Judgement 174, 177, 178–258, 211
Jung 80
Justice 113, 115, 204

K
Kaph 188
Karma 112
Kaunio, Marianne 9
King 251, 253
Knowing 110

L
Leo 88
Libra 94
Lie 155
Lion 88, 105
Lonely 95
Love 42
Lovers 64, 66, 200
Lunar cycle 33

M
Maat 113
Magician 26
Major Arcana 196–258
Man 105, 250
Manichean 80
Matthews, Caitlín 13, 191
Meditation
  Introductory 16
Melany, Jade 191
Merkaba 83
Merlin 26, 45, 59, 61, 90, 93
  Madness 61
Minor Arcana 189, 213–258, 218–258
Moko, Tapani 9
Monshin, Deborah 130
Moon 72, 164, 201, 210
Mother 42, 138, 249, 254
Musical 252
Mystics 122

N
Nature 81
Numbers 44, 51, 68, 82, 96
  Primal 95

O
Odin 123, 124
Opening 16
Orion 160
Orphic egg 174
Otherworld 164
Outer World 7
Owl 26

P

Palmer Hall, Manly 72
   Secret Teachings .. 76, 95
Pan 142
Past Life 130, 131
Pathworkings 15
Pentacles 215, 240–258, 256
Pillars 164
Pineal gland 175
Powers 76
Prince 254
Princess 253
Pyramid 183

Q

Queen 251

R

Regardie, Israel 64
Reiki 37
Relationship 248
Rider Waite 60

S

S.O.L I.N.V.I.C.T.U.S 173
Sacrifice 122
Sagittarius 140
Samsara 111
Saturn 186
Scientific 252
Seer 45
Sekhmet 113, 114
Separatio 154
Sephiroth 68
Sex 249, 250
Shadow lands 122
Shaitan 147
Shaman 59
Silver star 37
Smallness 90
Smith, Pamela Coleman 60
Solve et Coagula 68, 147
Son of the Mother 90
Sophia 36
Sothis 141, 157

Soul 44
Soulscapes 10
   Tarot 58
Spades 214
Spirit Guides 12
Star 157, 209
Stewart, R.J. 45
   Merlin, 71
Storm 214
Strength 202
Sun 131, 167, 170, 210
Swords 214, 224, 224–258

T

Taliesin 59, 60
Tarot For others 192–258
Teacher 57, 58
Temperance 135, 206
Tibetan 111
Time 186
Tower 149, 152, 208
Transitions 81
Tree of Life 68, 183
Triple goddess 36
Triskelion 45

U

Universe 182–258, 212

V

V.I.T.R.I.O.L 140
Venus 37, 42, 160
Vesica piscis 188

W

Wands 218
Western Mystery Tradition 14
Wheel of Fortune 105
Wife 249
Wise old man 56
World 182–258, 186–258
World Serpent 182

Z

Zodiac 108, 170

www.ingramcontent.com/pod-product-compliance
Lightning Source LLC
Chambersburg PA
CBHW040256170426
43192CB00020B/2818